CrimeScene
Science Fair Projects

CrimeScene
Science Fair Projects

Elizabeth Snoke Harris

LARK BOOKS

A Division of Sterling Publishing Co., Inc.
New York

Editor:
Rain Newcomb

Art Director:
Robin Gregory

Art Production Assistant:
Bradley Norris

Editorial Assistance:
Dawn Dillingham, Delores Gosnell, and Rose McLarney

Illustrator:
Orrin Lundgren

Photographer:
Steve Mann

Library of Congress Cataloging-in-Publication Data

Harris, Elizabeth Snoke, 1973-
  Crime scene science fair projects / by Elizabeth Snoke Harris. — 1st ed.
      p. cm.
  Includes index.
   ISBN 1-57990-765-2 (hardcover)
   1. Criminal investigation. 2. Forensic sciences. 3. Science projects. I.
Title.
HV8073.H29 2006
363.25'2—dc22

                                        2006016803

10 9 8 7 6 5 4 3 2 1

First Edition

Published by Lark Books, A Division of
Sterling Publishing Co., Inc.
387 Park Avenue South, New York, N.Y. 10016

Text © 2006, Elizabeth Snoke Harris
Photography © 2006, Lark Books
Illustrations © 2006, Lark Books

Distributed in Canada by Sterling Publishing,
c/o Canadian Manda Group, 165 Dufferin Street
Toronto, Ontario, Canada M6K 3H6

Distributed in the United Kingdom by GMC Distribution Services,
Castle Place, 166 High Street, Lewes, East Sussex, England BN7 1XU

Distributed in Australia by Capricorn Link (Australia) Pty Ltd.,
P.O. Box 704, Windsor, NSW 2756 Australia

If you have questions or comments about this book, please contact:
Lark Books
67 Broadway
Asheville, NC 28801
(828) 253-0467

Manufactured in China

ISBN 13: 978-1-57990-765-5
ISBN 10: 1-57990-765-2

For information about custom editions, special sales, premium and corporate
purchases, please contact Sterling Special Sales Department at 800-805-5489 or
specialsales@sterlingpub.com.

Contents

The CSI Effect

Have you noticed the first thing police do when they arrive at the scene of a crime? They put up barrier tape to secure the area. Behind that tape lays evidence—evidence forensic scientists will use to figure out exactly what happened.

Forensic scientists rush to the scene and look carefully at everything: tire prints, footprints, fingerprints, hair, blood, broken glass, tool marks, letters, notes, receipts, dirt—it's all evidence. Every drop of liquid and piece of lint has the potential to help the detectives piece together exactly what happened. So the forensic scientists collect what they find, take it back to the lab, and analyze it.

That's why, even as they help injured people get to the hospital or take suspects into custody, the police officers are careful not to disturb the crime scene behind that barrier tape. Walking in a crime scene is enough to change it and contaminate the evidence. Not only does contamination make it difficult to correctly analyze evidence, it can also make all of the evidence inadmissible in court.

Luckily, you aren't under the same pressure in a science fair. But the experiments you'll find in this book use the same techniques forensic scientists use to collect and examine evidence at a crime scene. With the scientific method, this book, and a few supplies, you can analyze blood spatter patterns, dust for fingerprints, figure out how to tell different types of pen inks apart, determine how a piece of ceramic was broken, and more. The only difference between your work and that of a forensic scientist is that you won't need any dead bodies to perform your experiments. (That would get you disqualified from your science fair.)

It's easy to make a great science fair project using this book. Begin by reading the next chapter, which covers everything you need to know. There you'll find out how to choose a topic that intrigues you, make a schedule for exploring it, design your experiment, and follow it through to its successful conclusion. You'll also find information on checking for errors in your experiment, analyzing the data, and turning it all into easy-to-understand charts and graphs.

Use the information in Chapter 1 to come up with your own project, or check out the forensic science projects that follow. Because you have to do the work and figure out the results, you can use any of these projects without having to worry about cheating on your homework! Just for fun, the projects section includes stories and trivia about forensic science careers, history, and more.

What is Forensic Science?

Forensics is anything that has to do with the law, which means that forensic science is just science applied to the law. Forensic scientists use science to help lawyers, police officers, investigators, and even judges solve crimes and catch criminals. There are specific types of forensic science such as forensic chemistry, forensic biology, forensic geology, forensic dentistry, and forensic entomology (the study of bugs). There are even forensic accountants. (Who do you think figures out how to arrest all the mobsters for tax evasion?) Forensic scientists can study and analyze everything (and I mean everything!) at a crime scene to figure out what happened. They don't just look for *fingerprints* and *DNA* samples, but they also examine dirt, pollen, footprints, glass, handwriting, chemicals, fibers, hair, insects, and more.

The earliest forensic scientists, like the fictional detective Sherlock Holmes, used careful observation and their knowledge of how the world works to deduce who committed the crime being investigated. Forensic scientists today still use knowledge and careful observation, but they also have access to tools such as infrared microscopes and electrophoresis equipment. Unfortunately, this doesn't necessarily make things easier, it just means there is more evidence to analyze!

Forensic science is used to catch the bad guys—but you want to be absolutely certain who the bad guys are. This means you'll need to perform your experiments many times to make sure your findings are correct without a shadow of a doubt. If you're trying to make generalizations, such as "the handwriting of all lefthanders slants left," you'll need to try out your *hypothesis* on lots of different people to make sure that your findings are true for everyone, not just a couple of people. If you're trying to narrow down suspects to one individual, such as by comparing fingerprints, you'll need to be as careful as possible and compare your findings to lots of other people to make sure your results are unique.

Discover Your Inner Forensic Scientist

In order to be a good scientist, you need to make careful observations and ask lots of questions. Take a good look at the room around you. A good forensic scientist could figure out who had been in the room, when he had been there, and what he'd been up to. What evidence can you see that could help you answer these questions? What can you do about the evidence you can't see? The experiments in this book will help you become more aware of clues on the ground, in the air, on your clothes, and even on the paper you use for your homework.

Secrets of Success

So, what is the secret to a fabulous science fair project, anyway? Well, there are three of them:

1. Come up with a fun, original question that you are really excited about.

You've probably got lots of these stuck up in your head. The steps on pages 11 to 13 will help you get them out of your head and into your Science Fair Lab Notebook.

2. Follow the scientific method to find an answer to your question.

The *scientific method* is a set of guidelines that scientists (like you!) use to answer their fascinating questions (see Secret #1). Don't sweat the details right now. I'll walk you through each step in the section on pages 13 to 16.

3. Do the best work you can do.

This is the most important part of your science fair project. It isn't hard and requires no special equipment. Just work as carefully and as methodically as you can. Your best will come out!

Plan of Action

Your science fair project is simply another way to explore the world around you—only this time with a plan. Just as no criminal mastermind would set out to commit the crime of the century without a master scheme, a good scientist wouldn't start an experiment without a well-thought-out plan. A good plan of action will cut down on the time it takes to do your experiment, ensure more accurate results, and allow another scientist to duplicate your experiment to verify your results. This section will tell you everything you need to know to come up with a foolproof method for your science fair project.

Get a Notebook

This is the very first thing you need to do. This will be your lab notebook, and it will ONLY be used for your science fair project. Any type of notebook will do, as long as it has paper and a cover to keep things such as water, chemicals, and your little sister from getting inside. Put your name on it, and if you like, write some intimidating warning to keep other people out. Anytime you do anything related to your project (and this includes middle-of-the-night "what if…" thoughts), write it down in your notebook. Be sure to keep your lab notebook handy.

Make a Schedule

Hopefully, you're not reading this book the night before the fair and you've given yourself some time to do your project. Find out when the fair is and mark it on a calendar. Figure out how much time you have to work on your project and make a schedule. Ideally, you should have about eight weeks to do your project. This might sound like a long time, but remember Secret #3? (See the box above.) Figure out whether your project is going to require collecting insects, recruiting lots of volunteers, or other time-sensitive activities. Take this

Checklist for Success:
Eight-Week Schedule Checklist

If you have eight weeks before the science fair, you can use this schedule as is. Check off each task as you complete it. Go ahead—it feels good—and it gives you a real sense of accomplishment. Write the dates in the spaces provided and get to work. If you have more than eight weeks, don't wait. Simply give yourself more time to do some of the tasks. Or get started and finish early. Hey, why not?!

Week # 1 (dates:_____)
- ⚪ Choose your topic.
- ⚪ Organize your notebook.
- ⚪ Ask questions.

Week #2 (dates:_____)
- ⚪ Research your chosen topic.

Week #3 (dates:_____)
- ⚪ Finish your research.
- ⚪ Figure out your question.
- ⚪ Develop your hypothesis.
- ⚪ Design your experiment.

Week #4 (dates:_____)
- ⚪ Turn in an experiment summary to your teacher.
- ⚪ Gather all the materials you need for your experiment.
- ⚪ Start your experiment.

Week #5 (dates:_____)
- ⚪ Set up an outline for your project report.
- ⚪ Continue your experiment.
- ⚪ Begin collecting materials for your display.

Week #6 (dates:_____)
- ⚪ Continue your experiment.
- ⚪ Write the first draft of your project report.
- ⚪ Sketch some designs for your display.

Week #7 (dates:_____)
- ⚪ Finish your experiment.
- ⚪ Revise the list of materials needed for the experiment

and the steps of the procedure, if necessary.
- ⚪ Analyze your data and draw your conclusion.
- ⚪ Revise the project report.

Week #8 (dates:_____)
- ⚪ Complete your display.
- ⚪ Edit and type the final draft of the project report.
- ⚪ Prepare for the fair.

The Fair (date:_____)

into account! Try to finish your experiment a week or two before the fair so you have time to write your report and make your display. Most important, make sure the schedule is realistic and you can actually stick to it.

While you're at it, it wouldn't hurt to get a copy of the rules to make sure you know what you're supposed to do. Some science fairs only let you do biology projects or won't let you do anything using animals. If you're doing an experiment that involves people, make sure you get written permission from the parents of anyone who's under 18. Figure this out now rather than after you've done six or eight weeks of work.

Pick a Topic

Since you'll be working on your project for at least two months, the topic should be something you really like. Picking a topic is much less intimidating than it seems. All you really need to do to pick a topic is think and write. (You might already know exactly what you want to do, but it never hurts to have a couple of backup ideas in case something doesn't work out.)

First, think of things you like to do. What are your hobbies? What are you interested in? What do you enjoy doing? Since you're reading this book, you'll probably put forensic science at the top of the list. Open up your lab notebook and write these things down on the first page. It doesn't matter how silly or crazy they sound; you're just getting a starting point.

If you're still having trouble, look around and pay attention to what you do every day. Look through the newspaper and talk to your friends and family. You've got lots of great resources right in front of you. Make a list of these things in your lab notebook.

Now that you have a list of potential topics, it's time to narrow it down a little. If you wrote down "crime," cross it out and write down what type of crimes you're interested in. Is it car theft, forgery, or attempted poisoning? If you wrote down "footprints," write down what aspect of footprints you're interested in. Do you want to figure out whose feet they come from, what the person who left them looked like, or what she was doing when she left them?

Take another look at the list. Pick one of the topics you have written down to be the basis for your project. (This is the hard part.) Keep the list around, though, since the odds are you'll be doing another science fair project next year, and it might come in handy.

Congratulations! You have a topic.

Research Time

Now you're ready to research your topic. Write down everything you already know about the topic in your lab notebook. What do you like best about it? Go to the library and check out some books (and actually read them). Find some experts on the topic and talk to them. Your friends and family might have information to share as well. Make sure you write down in your lab notebook what sources you're looking at (books, magazines, etc.), who you talk to, and all the interesting facts you come across.

Once you know a little more about your topic, you can start thinking up questions.

Good science questions usually come in a specific form. For instance:

How does _____ affect _____ ?

How does _____ compare to _____ ?

How does _____ determine _____ ?

You just need to fill in the blanks.

Picking a Question

Obviously, you need to have some questions before you can pick just one. Pull out that handy lab notebook again and write down every question you can think of about the topic you chose. Right now, you just need a bunch of questions. It doesn't matter whether they're good, bad, or really easy to answer. I'll help you fix that later. If you get stuck trying to think up questions, look back at the notes you took from your research. It doesn't really matter how many questions you think of, but three is a good number to aim for. Make sure the questions can't be answered with a simple yes or no answer.

For example, suppose you chose footprints as your topic. Some questions could be:

How are footprints made?

How do you match a foot to the footprint it made?

Can you tell how fast someone is walking from her footprints?

Now look at your list of questions and ask yourself,

"Can I measure something to help answer one of these questions?"

Looking at the list of footprint questions, only the last one has something you can easily measure: walking speed. This question looks promising, so you can explore it further.

So, let's look at our footprint question again to see whether we can use it to fill in the blanks of one of the questions in the box on page 12.

How does <u>the speed someone walks</u> affect <u>the space between their footprints?</u>

I think we have a winner!

The answer to this question could be useful to forensic scientists who observe footprints at a crime scene and are trying to reconstruct the crime. A criminal who walks slowly may not be familiar with her surroundings, while a criminal who walks quickly may be rushing because she didn't plan the crime ahead of time.

If you can't make one of your questions into a project, scratch it and pick another question. (That's why you wrote down more than one.)

Get Started with the Scientific Method

The scientific method is a set of guidelines that scientists use to help them answer questions. It's pretty straightforward, and you've already done the first two steps: researched and identified a problem. Now you just need to form a hypothesis, design an experiment, perform the experiment, and analyze the results.

It's simple. Take good notes in your lab notebook. Write down what you do, how you do it, and what you see. What seems like a silly observation at the time might be very important later. Draw lots of pictures, too. (It doesn't matter if you can't draw. You aren't being judged on your artistic ability.) Label different parts of the sketch to make it clear what you've drawn.

Form a Hypothesis

The first step is to make a hypothesis. A hypothesis is just a guess at the answer to your question. All you need to do is take your question and make it into an answer.

Examples:

I think _____ will affect _____.

OR

I think _____ will not affect _____.

I believe _____ will determine _____.

OR

I believe _____ will not determine _____.

Don't stress out about whether your guess is right or wrong. At this stage, it doesn't matter. You haven't done your experiment, so you aren't supposed to know the answer—yet. Besides, you might learn more if what actually happens is not what you expected. It's okay if your final results don't support your hypothesis. The science fair judges won't count off for this. (Just make sure you can explain to them why you chose the hypothesis you did!)

Using our footprint example, one hypothesis might be:

I think the speed someone walks will determine the space between their footprints.

See how easy that was?

Design Your Experiment

At this point, you might think you're ready to jump in and start working on your experiment, but you're wrong. It'll save a lot of time later if you make a game plan first. You guessed it—pull out that lab notebook and start scribbling. There are three basic parts to your experiment.

1. The Independent Variable

The *independent variable* is what you change in the experiment. You're in charge of how it changes, and it doesn't depend on anything else. This is usually the same thing that's in the first blank of your question from page 12. In our case, that would be the speed you walk. Make sure you only have ONE independent variable. If you're testing more than one thing at a time, it'll be very difficult to draw an accurate conclusion.

Now that you know what you're going to change, you need to decide how you're going to change it. How fast will you walk? How many different speeds will you walk? How will you measure the speed? (You might need to refer to your research to make these decisions.) Speed is distance divided by time, so you'll measure the time it takes you to walk a set distance. You could walk very slowly, at a medium pace, and as fast as you can. That will give you three different speeds to walk. You can always go back and add more *trials* if you don't get enough information to answer the question.

Also think about how many trials you're going to run at each speed. That is, how many times will you walk and record the distance between footprints at each speed? Doing more trials helps get rid of *random error* (see page 22 for more information on random error). Three trials are acceptable, but more is better. That means for each of the three walking speeds, you should walk at least three times. So, if you have three different speeds and you're running three trials at each time, you'll be walking nine times. That's a lot of walking! You might want to wear your good walking shoes.

2. The Dependent Variable

Decide what you're going to measure and how you're going to measure it. What you're going to measure is also known as the *dependent variable*. It's called that because it depends on what happens to your independent variable. In other words, when you change your independent variable, your dependent variable will change too. This is the same thing that's in the second blank of your question on page 12 (gee, that sure is coming in handy!). In our case, that would be the distance between the footprints. You can measure this using a ruler or meter stick once you decide what exactly you're going to measure: toe to heel, toe to toe, or heel to heel. Measuring your dependent variable might not always be so simple. You may need to design an *apparatus,* which is an unusual piece of equipment or tool, or use an instrument such as a thermometer, ruler, or stopwatch to take the measurement. In this case, you need to figure out how to leave footprints on the ground so there is something to measure.

3. The Controls

Finally, you need to decide what other variables you're going to control. That is, what other factors might affect the distance between footprints? Make sure that these don't change during the experiment. These things are your *controls.* Some variables to control might be the

person doing the walking, the type of shoe she's wearing, if any, and the surface she's walking on. That's a lot of stuff to keep track of. Write it all down in your lab notebook. (That'll keep you from forgetting anything AND impress the judges!)

Do Your Experiment

This is the part you've been waiting for! Gather your materials together, call up a couple of helpers if you need them, and get to it. Just remember to work slowly and carefully and be aware of what you're doing. A sloppy experiment is not the way to science fair fame.

Use your lab notebook while you're working. Write down your measurements neatly in it so you don't have to redo the experiment later. Be sure to note any adjustments you make to your design and any observations that you didn't expect. Take pictures and draw diagrams. But most of all, have fun!

Do the Math

Now that you've done your experiment, you've got a bunch of numbers—*data,* if you want to be scientific about it. You need to turn those numbers into something you can use to answer your question. *Average* your trials for each walking speed. Visualize your data using a graph (see pages 20 and 21 for help with this). This will make the next step much easier.

Analyze Your Data

At this point, you've got some results, but what does it all mean? Do you see any patterns? How did the dependent variable (distance between footprints) change as you varied the independent variable (walking speed)? Are there any *outliers,* or really weird data points that don't fit in with the rest of your measurements? You might consider throwing these away or retaking that measurement.

If you're having trouble at this step, you might want to consider retaking some measurements or trying something a little different with your procedure. It's okay to go back and adjust the way you take a measurement or set up the equipment. Just write it down in your notebook.

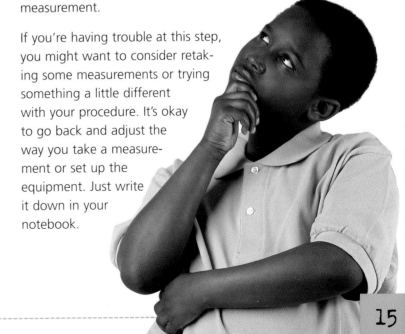

Draw a Conclusion

Now it's time to answer your question. What does the data tell you? Is your hypothesis supported or not? A hypothesis is never right or wrong. Someone could design another experiment that contradicts your hypothesis even if your experiment supports it, and you could both be right. Science is more complex than right and wrong answers. Generally, the process you take to reach your conclusion is just as important as the conclusion.

If you can't answer your question from the data, don't freak out! Don't try to force an answer out of nothing. Can you collect more data or do another experiment to find the answer? The science fair judges won't mind if you can't find an answer as long as your experiment is done well and you have a plan for further experiments. (Mmmm, sounds like a project for next year!)

Prepare for the Fair

Congratulations! You've answered your science fair question and learned something. Now it's time to share your findings with the rest of the world. Most science fairs require a written report and a display. Here are some tips to make doing both of these things easy.

Write Your Report

This is simple—just look in your lab notebook! All of these sections are probably already written down in there somewhere; it's just a matter of finding the information.

Title Page

This should be short and to the point. Your title shouldn't be longer than your report. Be sure to include your name, grade, the date, and your school on the title page.

Abstract

An *abstract* gives people an idea of what your project is about. All you need are a couple of sentences that say what your project is about and what you found out.

Introduction

The introduction is where you explain what your project is all about. What question are you trying to answer? How did you choose this topic? Why is this an important subject to study? You might also want to include important background information you found in your research.

How Did You Do Your Experiment?

Think of this section as a story about how you did your experiment rather than instructions for doing it again. Describe what you did, what you measured, and what

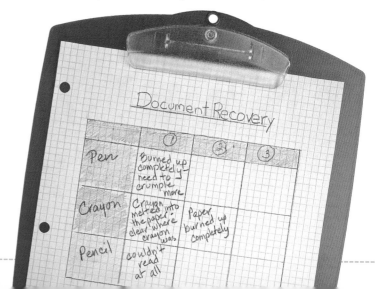

The Forensic Science of Footprints and What They Mean

DATA

MATERIALS

PROBLEM

HYPOTHESIS

VARIABLES

Conclusion

Here's your chance to explain what it all means and give the answer to your question. Is there anything you would do differently? Did you come up with more questions than answers? What are some ideas for further research?

Put Together Your Display

For the actual science fair, you'll need a display. This is usually a three-paneled, freestanding board that you can buy at most office and school supply stores. Be sure to check your science fair rules for restrictions on space and size for your display so you don't get disqualified! Here are some tips for making a super display:

Less is More

Don't make your board too wordy. Use lists instead of paragraphs where possible (such as your procedure and conclusions). Leave something to talk about with the judges.

Use Pictures

If you can use pictures instead of words to show your procedure and setup clearly, then do it! However, don't include extra, unrelated pictures just for decoration. Be sure to label the important parts of a picture or diagram that you want the judges to notice. If you use pictures from someone else, like from a book or the Internet, be sure to give them credit.

Keep It Simple

Make sure your board isn't crowded. Empty space is a good thing. Also, pay attention to the colors you choose. Don't put pink words on a blue background or do anything that will make the judges cross-eyed.

Your display board should include the following things:

- ○ Title
- ○ Problem/Question
- ○ Hypothesis
- ○ Abstract
- ○ Description/Drawing/Photo of experimental setup
- ○ Procedure
- ○ Data, including graphs and tables (but graphs are usually better)
- ○ Conclusions

---

materials you used. What were your dependent and independent variables? What were your controls and how did you control them? Include any problems you ran into and describe how you dealt with them. This is also a good place to put a drawing or photo of your setup. Be sure to label all the parts.

Data

This is where you put your graphs and data tables. However, if you made a graph of your data, you don't need a table with the same data. (See pages 20 and 21 for more information about charts and graphs.) Make sure you have the appropriate labels. Don't forget the units of measurement.

Discuss Your Data

What do your graphs and tables show? Point out any patterns or trends you want the reader (or the judges) to notice.

Keep It Neat

Use a computer, word processor, or stencils to print out all the parts of your display so you don't have to worry about handwriting. Use rubber cement to attach paper to your board. (Glue can make the paper look crumpled.) Don't use staples; most boards aren't thick enough to hold them.

Before you glue everything down, have other folks (especially people who didn't help you perform the experiment) look at your display. Ask them if they can read everything, if it makes sense, and if anything is missing.

Check the Rules!

If you plan on including your apparatus, instruments, chemicals or other items with your display, check to make sure the rules allow this. Animals, in particular, even fish and insects, are usually restricted.

Tips for Talking to the Judges

- Talk slowly and clearly.
- Don't read off your display.
- Explain why you picked your topic and how you chose your hypothesis.
- Describe what everything is and how it relates to your experiment.
- Point out patterns in your data, graphs, or charts.
- Remember that the judges are on your side. They want to see how well you have done.
- Relax and smile!

Above all, be honest. Don't try to cover up the errors you made. Explain what they were and how you would do things differently if you had more time. If you don't know the answer to a question, that's okay! It's better to admit you don't know than to try to make something up. (The judges will know.) Offer to look up the answer and send it to them later. Be proud of the good work you have done.

Before You Go to the Fair

- Being prepared for the fair will help you have a good time.

- Double-check the rules one more time for what you're allowed to bring. Check the date, time, and place while you're at it.

• Practice. Have your parents or friends pretend to be judges, and practice talking about your project. If you can explain your experiment to your grandmother, then you can explain it to anyone!

• Gather everything together that you're going to bring to the fair, such as your display, notebook, and any approved apparatus from your project that you might like to show the judges.

• Dress nicely. Don't wear a hat or sloppy clothes. It won't hurt to make a good impression.

While You're There

Relax! You've done everything you can, so now just enjoy the fair. Each fair is different. You might need to stand by your project the whole time and talk to all sorts of people about the project. You might not even know which ones are the judges! At some fairs, the judges just look at the displays and don't even talk to the scientists. It's always better to get a chance to talk to the judges so they can see how important your project is to you.

You're going to be explaining your project to everyone who walks by, including the judges. You can use the report you wrote to help make your presentation. But don't just read your report! Talk to the people who come up to your display. Start with your abstract, then walk them through your hypothesis, procedure, data, and conclusions, then summarize what you just said in a couple of sentences. Mention any interesting questions that came up during your experiment. What would you like to investigate next on this problem?

Science Fair Safety

When in doubt, ask for help. If you're not sure that you can handle a part of the experiment by yourself, it's all right to get an adult helper. This is especially true when you're dealing with candles, household chemicals, or the stove. Some experiments in this book will require an adult helper.

 Wear goggles if you're working with liquids, fire, or anything that can fly through the air. This is particularly important if you wear contact lenses. Some acids can actually melt your contact lens onto your eyeball!

 Always wear closed-toe shoes like sneakers or shoes that tie. No flip-flops or sandals! You don't want to drop anything heavy or spill anything dangerous onto your feet.

 Read the labels on household chemicals for safety warnings and important protective measures such as wearing gloves.

 No eating or drinking in the lab. Even if you're in the kitchen, do not eat while doing science. The food can contaminate the experiment, and the experiment can contaminate you!

 Clean up before and after your experiment. Be sure your workspace is clean before you start, and don't leave a mess when you are done.

 Keep the TV and radio off. Loud music and TV shows can be distracting. To do good science and prevent dangerous mistakes, you want to be sure you can focus while you work.

Charts, Graphs & Tables

Charts and graphs are a great way to present your data, not just because they look good on a display board but also because they organize your data in ways that can be understood easily and quickly. There are many different ways to create graphs and tables. Pick the right way to display the type of data you have. Here are the four most common examples.

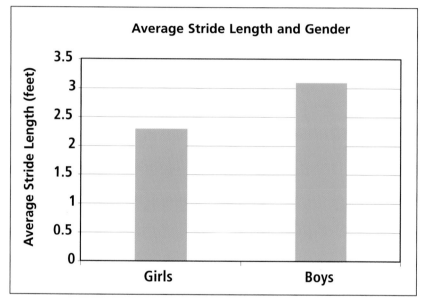

Average Stride Length and Gender

(Bar graph: vertical axis labeled "Average Stride Length (feet)" from 0 to 3.5 in increments of 0.5; horizontal axis shows "Girls" bar at about 2.25 and "Boys" bar at about 3.1)

Helpful hint: *Although they look cool, avoid 3D graphs and extra wide or narrow bars. They can distort your data and make it difficult to compare values.*

Data Tables

You've collected lots of numbers and you want to show them all off. A data table seems like the best way to do this. Think again. Data tables should be used sparingly. Although they are perfect for collecting your data, when preparing for your display board, a big table of numbers can seem overwhelming and confusing. However, if you have four or less numbers, a data table isn't such a bad idea.

When you put your table together, be sure to label each column of data and include the units of measurement. Don't forget a title too. The left-hand column should contain your *independent variable,* while the columns to the right contain your *dependent variables.*

Bar Graph

When your data is *nominal,* that is, your independent variables are names or things rather than amounts, a bar graph is the way to go. For example, you can use a bar graph to look at the stride length of boys and girls or to compare how different classes did on a social studies test. Bar graphs are used mostly to compare a set of measurements. The horizontal axis should always contain the independent variable and the vertical axis shows the dependent variable or what you measured. Be sure to label the axes and don't forget the units of measurement too.

Line Graph

A line graph is perfect if your data is *ordinal*. This means your independent variable is a number or an amount such as age. Line graphs are also used to show patterns or changes over time. Just like with a bar graph, the horizontal axis should always contain the independent variable and the vertical axis shows the dependent variable or what you measured. Be sure to label the axes and don't forget the units of measurement too. If you have multiple sets of data on the same graph, use different colors or symbols for the different sets of data.

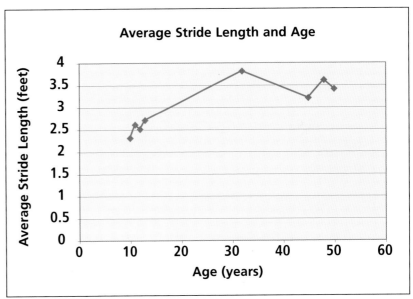

Helpful hint: *Too many lines on a graph can be confusing, especially if they overlap. Try to find the simplest graph that makes your point.*

Pie Chart

Pie charts are used to show percentages or fractions. They are sometimes called circle graphs too. The whole circle (or pie) equals 100 percent and the different piece of the pie make up the whole. Pie charts do not show changes over time. For example, you could use a pie chart to show which foot your subjects took their first step with. Be sure to include a title and a legend for deciphering the graph.

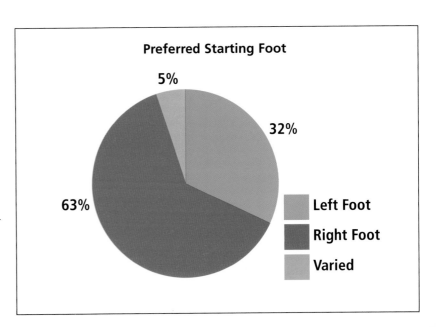

Error

Let's face it, no scientist is perfect, not even you. Every experiment is going to have some sort of error. The key to dealing with error is to find it and point it out before other folks (like the judges) can call you on it.

Error can affect how accurate and precise your measurements are. While these two words are used together a lot, they actually mean very different things.

Precision means that the measurements are always close together. Accuracy means that the measurements are close to the true or real value.

You can be precise and not accurate or accurate and not precise. Your goal is to be both!

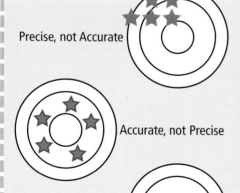

Precise, not Accurate

Accurate, not Precise

Accurate and Precise

There are two types of error that will affect the accuracy and precision of your data.

Systematic error is caused when you do the same thing wrong every time. Most of the time you don't even know it, because hopefully if you did you would stop doing it! Systematic error usually causes problems with *accuracy*.

Random error is when factors, usually out of your control, affect your measurement differently each time. Sometimes you might measure low and other times high. You can still get an accurate reading, but it won't be very *precise*.

Your job is to get rid of both systematic and random error so that your measurements are precise and accurate. When writing your report and talking to judges, it's important to be as specific as possible about where error might have popped up in your experiment. Here are some things to look for:

Mistakes

Of course these are going to cause errors. You can prevent these by working slowly and carefully. Don't be afraid to redo a measurement if you think you made a mistake.

Human Error

This gets confused with mistakes a lot because humans are usually the ones making mistakes. However, human error has to do with the fact that we don't have perfect vision and steady hands all the time. Human error can also occur if you haven't had a lot of practice using a measuring instrument.

Instrument Error

Most of your measuring devices have a bit of error built into them. If your ruler only has marks every millimeter, then the smallest you can measure, no matter how hard you try, is 0.5 millimeters. You may also want to take a close look at your ruler while you're at it. Make sure the end is really 0 millimeters. Sometimes rulers (and other instruments) get worn or are printed wrong so the end is not exactly 0.

Observing the System

Taking a measurement can change what you are measuring! When you place a thermometer in a container of hot liquid, the cool thermometer might actually lower the temperature of the liquid while you measure its temperature. Be careful when you're working with people—they might behave differently when they know they are being studied.

Sampling

The more data you collect, the less likely you are to have random error. If you take only one measurement, there's no way to know if it's accurate or not. If you average lots of values (at least three, but more is better) then you have a better chance of getting an accurate value.

The Projects

The projects in the next five chapters explore different applications of forensic science.

If the project requires adult supervision or assistance, there will be an **Adult Supervision** icon 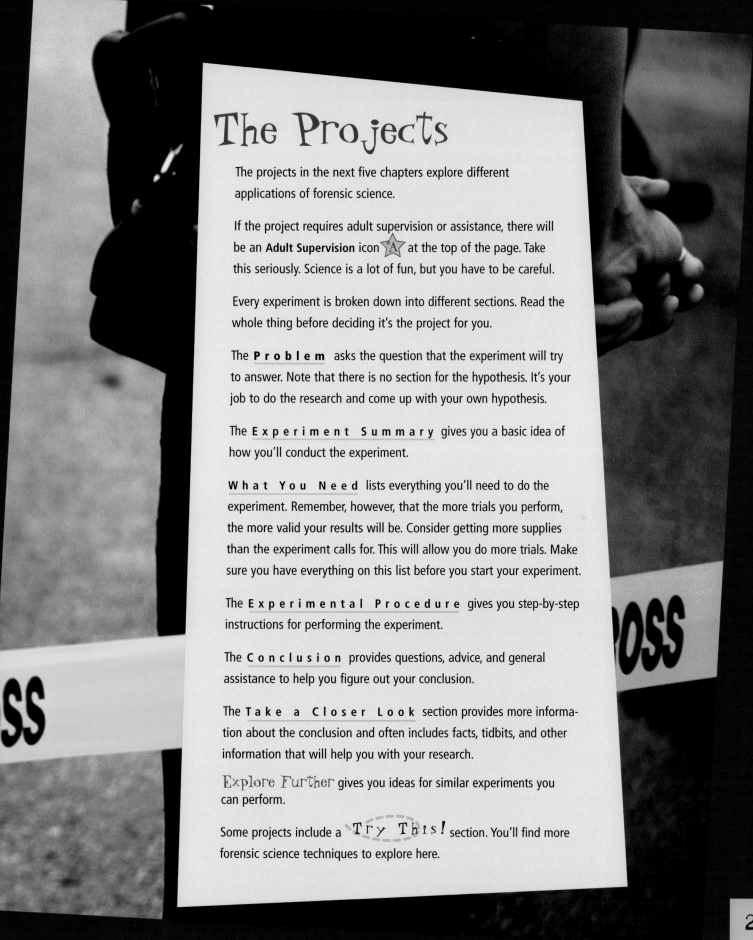 at the top of the page. Take this seriously. Science is a lot of fun, but you have to be careful.

Every experiment is broken down into different sections. Read the whole thing before deciding it's the project for you.

The **Problem** asks the question that the experiment will try to answer. Note that there is no section for the hypothesis. It's your job to do the research and come up with your own hypothesis.

The **Experiment Summary** gives you a basic idea of how you'll conduct the experiment.

What You Need lists everything you'll need to do the experiment. Remember, however, that the more trials you perform, the more valid your results will be. Consider getting more supplies than the experiment calls for. This will allow you do more trials. Make sure you have everything on this list before you start your experiment.

The **Experimental Procedure** gives you step-by-step instructions for performing the experiment.

The **Conclusion** provides questions, advice, and general assistance to help you figure out your conclusion.

The **Take a Closer Look** section provides more information about the conclusion and often includes facts, tidbits, and other information that will help you with your research.

Explore Further gives you ideas for similar experiments you can perform.

Some projects include a **Try This!** section. You'll find more forensic science techniques to explore here.

Blood & Guts

The physical evidence of a violent crime can be gruesome—
and challenging for a forensic scientist to find and identify.
Investigators collect anything that could help them determine
what happened, especially substances that might be human.
All of this goes back to the lab to be analyzed. If a scientist
identifies the substance as human, she can use DNA tests to
determine who left it at the crime scene, and how.

Blood Spatter Patterns

When blood is found at a crime scene, the pattern made by the drops can tell investigators what happened. The blood spatter changes, depending on the amount of blood, the angle at which it hits the ground, the speed of the droplets, and the distance from which the blood drops.

Problem

How does the shape of blood spatters vary with the distance dropped?

Experiment Summary

You'll drip fake blood from different heights and measure the resulting spatter pattern.

What You Need

- ◯ Paper
- ◯ Hard, flat surface
- ◯ Fake blood (see the recipe on page 26)
- ◯ Dropper
- ◯ Yardstick
- ◯ Camera (optional)

Fake Blood Recipe

What You Need

- 4 tablespoons clear corn syrup
- 2 tablespoons water
- 4 drops red food coloring
- $\frac{1}{8}$ teaspoon cornstarch
- $\frac{1}{8}$ teaspoon cocoa
- Resealable sandwich bag

What You Do

1. Add the corn syrup, water, food coloring, cornstarch, and cocoa to the sandwich bag and close it tightly.

2. Squish the bag with your fingers until the blood is thoroughly mixed.

Fake Blood

Experimental Procedure

1. Place a piece of paper on a hard, flat surface. This should be somewhere easy to clean, such as the kitchen floor, since the blood spatters may make a mess.

2. Fill the dropper with the fake blood. Place the bottom of the yardstick on the paper and use it to measure 12 inches up from the ground. Carefully drip one drop of blood onto the paper from this height.

3. Measure and record the diameter of the *blood spatter pattern* (BSP) and any other observations you may have. You may wish to take a photograph or make a sketch of the BSP.

4. Repeat step 2 at least five more times with a clean piece of paper at a height of 12 inches and calculate the average diameter of the BSP.

5. Repeat steps 2 through 4 for heights of 18, 24, 30, 36, 42, and 48 inches.

Conclusion

Make a graph of the BSP diameter and height dropped. Is there a relationship between diameter and height? Predict the diameter for blood dropped from 60 inches and test your prediction. Why do you think the BSP diameter changes as the height changes?

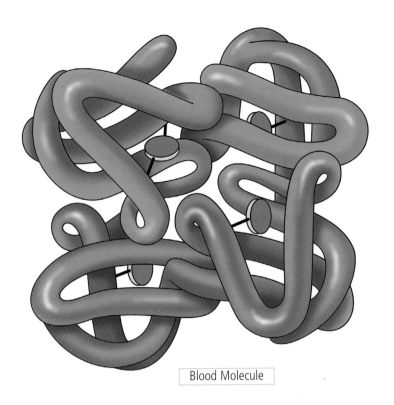

Blood Molecule

out of an artery or flung off by a shake of the arm. Combination spatters contain elements of both impact and projection spatters.

Blood is a mixture of solids (red and white blood cells and platelets) dissolved in a liquid (plasma). The fake blood you made has the same *viscosity* (flow) and density as blood before it *clots*. When blood leaves the body, it clots within a few minutes. Clotting is when the solid parts clump together, stopping the flow of blood. The liquid part that is left is called *serum*. Serum is just the plasma without the proteins that help the blood clot. Serum looks like a yellowish liquid; clotted blood looks like dark jelly. Investigators use the amount of clotting that has taken place in the blood found at a crime scene to estimate the time since the bleeding started.

Take a Closer Look

When blood leaves the body in a drop, it gains speed as it falls. The farther the drop has to fall, the faster it's going when it hits the ground. The greater speed increases the diameter of the BSP. Greater speeds also affect the edges of drops in the BSP. Fast-moving drops produce scalloped edges. If the drop of blood is falling even faster, it bounces off the paper and splashes back down, making a ring of smaller drops around the edge of the main spatter. If the drop hits the surface straight on, it forms a circle. Changing the angle of impact elongates the BSP into an oval. The pointiest end of the oval is directed in the drop's direction of travel.

Investigators look at all of the blood drops in the room, evaluating their size, distribution, and shape to reconstruct what happened. They classify BSP by speed (low, medium, or high), which indicates what may have caused the BSP. Investigators also classify BSP by the type of pattern. Impact spatters occur when something hits the body, like a fist or a knife. Projection spatters result from blood that is sprayed

Explore Further

Try altering other factors that affect the BSP.

Amount of blood: Increase the hole size on the dropper.

Angle of impact: Place the paper on a piece of cardboard propped up on one end by books. Use a protractor to measure the angle with the floor. This measurement is the angle of impact. Compare the BSP of very low angles, like 10 or 20 degrees, to very steep angles, like 70 or 80 degrees.

Motion: How will the BSP change if whatever is dripping the blood is moving? Lay out a row of papers about 9 feet (3 meters) long. Walk at different speeds as you drop the blood. Have someone time how long it takes you to walk the entire distance so you can calculate your average speed. Try walking slowly and quickly while you drop the blood.

Surface: Drop the blood on different surface. Does it form a different pattern on glass than it does on concrete or paper?

Is It Blood?

You arrive at a crime scene and see splatters of a dark liquid on the ground. How do you know for sure if it's blood? Hemastix are used to test substances to see if they contain hemoglobin, a component of blood, but sometimes they may give a false positive. That is, they will indicate that blood is present when it really isn't. Forensic scientists need to know what types of substances give this result so they can be sure that their results are accurate.

Problem

How do different substances affect the results of a test for blood?

Experiment Summary

You'll test several substances with Hemastix and compare the results to real blood.

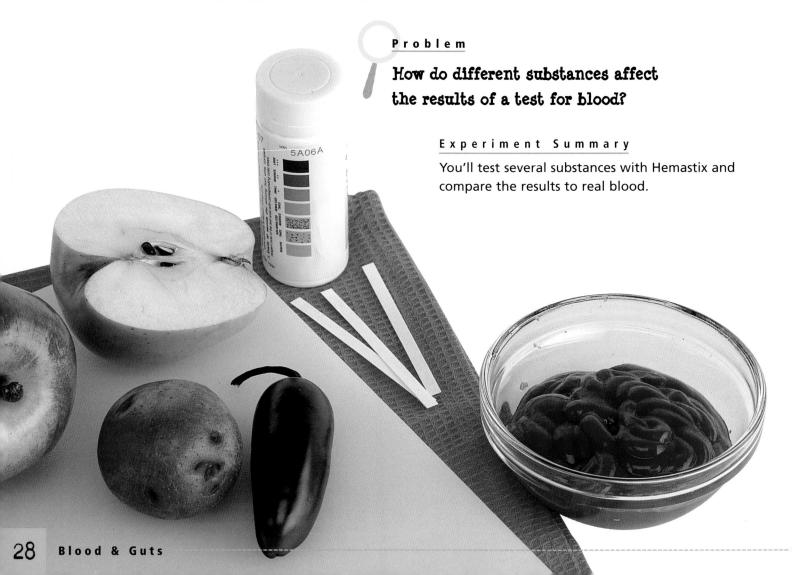

What You Need

- ○ **Cotton swabs**
- ○ **Distilled water**
- ○ **Blood (use the juice on the bottom of the tray meat comes in)***
- ○ **Hemastix (can be found or ordered from most drug stores in packs of 50 or more)**
- ○ **Bleach**
- ○ **Ammonia**
- ○ **Copper Sulfate (bluestone algecide for cleaning pools)**
- ○ **Potassium Permanganate (clearwater for aquariums)**
- ○ **Apple**
- ○ **Jalapeño pepper**
- ○ **Green onion**
- ○ **Red potato**
- ○ **White potato**
- ○ **Ketchup**
- ○ **Red food coloring**
- ○ **Anything else you want to test**

*Wash your hands well with soap after handling meat and blood.

Experimental Procedure

1. Wet a cotton swab with distilled water and dip the tip of the swab in the blood.

2. Press the swab against the indicator end of the Hemastix.

3. Wait 10 seconds. Observe and record the color change. The blood will give a true positive, so the indicator on the Hemastix should turn from orange to a greenish blue. Label and save the Hemastix so you can compare it to your other results. Wash your hands.

4. Repeat steps 1 through 3, testing the other substances. Record your results. Label and save the Hemastix so you can compare them later. When you test the fruits and vegetables, test the skin, leaves, stems, seeds, and flesh separately. The different parts may give different results. If you can't tell if the Hemastix changes color, repeat the test.

Conclusion

Which substances gave a false positive for blood? Were all of your tests conclusive? That is, could you tell for sure if the Hemastix showed a color change? Rank the Hemastix in order from most like blood to least like blood. Did some parts of your fruits and vegetables give different results from others? For example, did the apple stem give the same result as inside the apple? How could your results be useful to a forensic scientist?

Ologies

Forensics is the use of science to analyze evidence to be used in a court of law. But what about these other words? Match the forensic-ologies with their definitions! (Well, not all of these are —ologies, but you get the idea.) All are areas of study that help forensic scientists solve crimes.

The study of ...

1. Anthropology
2. Ballistics
3. Criminology
4. Cryptology
5. Dactylography
6. Entomology
7. Odontology
8. Palynology
9. Pathology
10. Serology
11. Toxicology
12. Trichology
13. Fractography

A. Pollen
B. Insects
C. Poisons
D. Blood serum
E. Corpses
F. Hair
G. Projectiles (like bullets)
H. Fingerprints
I. Humans
J. Crime
K. Secret messages
L. Teeth
M. How things break

Answers:

1:I 2:G 3:J 4:K 5:H 6:B 7:L 8:A 9:E 10:D 11:C 12:F 13:M

Take a Closer Look

There are several tests that investigators use to identify blood at a crime scene. Hemastix is one of the simplest and quickest tests. It also doesn't require a large sample of blood to give an accurate result. On TV, you may see the investigators spray an area where they suspect blood is present with a chemical called Luminol that causes bloodstains to glow blue in the dark. This lets investigators photograph bloodstain patterns that can't be easily seen.

Once blood has been identified at a crime scene, investigators try to determine who it came from and how it got there. The first step to finding out whose blood was found is to determine the *blood type.* Most people have blood types that can be classified as A, B, O, or AB types. Blood typing can only eliminate suspects. That is, if blood of types A and O was found at the crime scene and a suspect has type AB, then we know that the suspect did not leave any blood at the scene. However, this doesn't mean he wasn't at the crime scene—he just wasn't bleeding!

The only way to tell for sure whom the blood at a crime scene belongs to is by using DNA fingerprinting. (This test is extremely expensive and is used only in the most violent and high profile cases.) There are two ways to determine a DNA fingerprint.

In RFLP *(restriction fragment length polymorphisms)* DNA is pulled out of a whole bunch of cells, such as from several drops of blood. Then the long strands of DNA are cut into pieces at specific points, giving scientists many small DNA strands. (Since everyone's DNA is different, every person will have different sized DNA pieces after they have been cut. Some of the DNA pieces will be short and others will be very long.) Next, DNA strands are run through an electrophoresis

quite accurate and precise, but it takes a long time. You can wait anywhere from three weeks to three months to get a result!

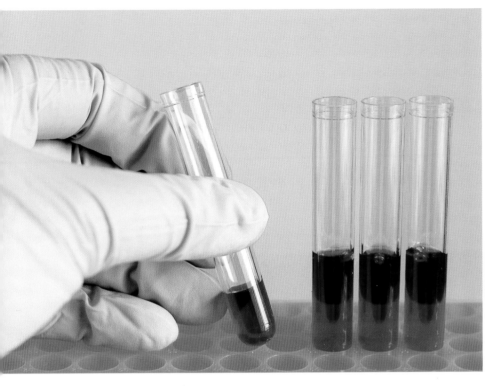

PCR (polymerase chain reaction) is very similar to RFLP except that it's used when there is a very small sample, such as a drop or two of blood. PCR breaks the DNA into pieces and then makes millions of copies of just part of the DNA strand. Specific markers in the smaller piece of DNA are then compared to see if two samples match. Even though PCR is not quite as precise as RFLP, it's much faster. It usually takes less than a week to get results. This method can also be used on older and smaller samples such as hair, fingernails, and even saliva from the back of used stamps!

gel. The gel is similar to a rectangular piece of gelatin with small holes or wells along one edge. All the DNA strands are placed in the wells and an electric current is run through the gel. The pieces of DNA will move through the gel with the current. The smaller pieces will move through the gel faster than the long pieces. This separates the DNA into two or more different "bands" that correspond to the different lengths of DNA pieces. Scientists then compare the pattern of bands in one DNA sample to the pattern of bands in another sample. If the samples come from the same person, the DNA will produce the same pattern of bands. The process is

Explore Further

How much blood is needed to indicate a reading on the Hemastix? Dilute the blood by mixing it with distilled water. Start your tests with a 1:2 dilution (1 drop of blood with 2 drops of water). Gradually increase the dilution (increase the number of water drops) until the Hemastix doesn't change color when you test it. This will tell you the sensitivity of the Hemastix test.

DNA Extraction

One of the most powerful tools for forensics scientists is DNA fingerprinting. But, before you can analyze someone's DNA, you need to pull it out of his cells. In fact, everything with cells has DNA, including the contents of your refrigerator!

Problem

How does the amount of DNA vary between different types of fruits and vegetables?

Experiment Summary

You'll extract DNA from various fruits and vegetables to compare the amount you get from each type.

What You Need

- 95 percent ethanol (also known as ethyl alcohol)
- Refrigerator
- Kiwi fruit
- Knife
- Food scale
- Food processor or blender
- Extraction solution (see the recipe on page 33)
- Measuring spoons
- Large mixing bowl of ice water
- Strainer
- Large, clean jar (a spaghetti or pickle jar works well)
- Pantyhose
- Large test tube with stopper or baby food jar
- Onion
- Spinach
- Strawberry
- Ruler
- Round toothpicks

1. Place the 95 percent ethanol in the fridge. You'll need it to be cold when you use it later.

2. Cut the kiwi fruit into pieces. Use the scale to measure 1 ounce of the fruit. Place the fruit in the food processor or blender.

3. Add 4 tablespoons (60 ml) of extraction solution to the kiwi fruit. Blend the kiwi thoroughly for about 5 minutes.

4. Place the container from the food processor or blender in the ice water to cool the kiwi mixture for one minute. Then blend the kiwi some more. Cool, then blend. Repeat this five times.

5. Place the strainer over the large jar and place a piece of pantyhose over the strainer. Filter the mixture through the pantyhose and strainer.

6. Pour 1 tablespoon (15 ml) of the filtered solution into the test tube.

7. Being careful not to shake the test tube, add 1 tablespoon (15 ml) of cold 95 percent ethanol to the test tube. Pour the ethanol along the side of the test tube so that it floats on top of the filtered solution.

8. Take a look at your test tube. The DNA is floating on the top portion of the liquid. Use your ruler to measure the height of this layer and record it in your lab notebook. After you've recorded your measurement, you can try to remove the DNA by twirling it around a toothpick if you want.

9. Thoroughly wash and dry the blender, test tube, and strainer. Then, repeat steps 2 through 8 with the kiwi fruit three more times. Average the measurements you recorded for the height of the DNA layer. This number will represent the amount of DNA extracted from the kiwi.

10. Repeat the process using the same amount of onion, spinach, and strawberry. Remember to wash your equipment thoroughly after each trial.

Conclusion

Make a bar graph of the amount of DNA vs. food. Which food yielded the most DNA? Research which plant has the greatest number of chromosomes to see if this matches your results. If not, why do you think that might be?

Extraction Solution Recipe

What You Need
- ½ cup (about 100 ml) shampoo*
- 1 tablespoon (20 g) table salt
- Container
- Water
- Spoon

*Do not use shampoo with conditioner or baby shampoo.

What You Do

1. Mix the shampoo and table salt together in the container.

2. Add water to make a final volume of 4¼ cups (1 liter). Dissolve the salt by stirring slowly to avoid foaming. This recipe will make enough solution to perform five extractions.

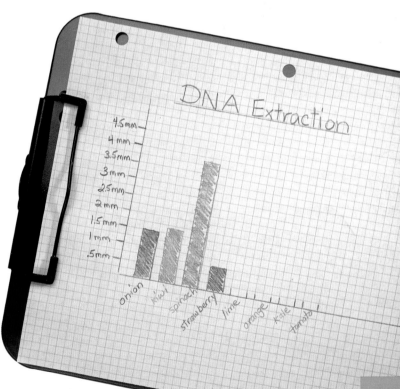

Try This!

Extracting Human DNA

It's difficult to extract as many of your own cells as there are in a whole kiwi fruit (without cutting off your hand and sticking it in the blender). You can't compare the DNA extracted from your cheek cells to that extracted from fruit and vegetables, but it's still fun to do! (And besides, you'll need both hands to perform this experiment.)

What You Need

○ Measuring spoons
○ Salt
○ Measuring cups

○ Water
○ Large test tube with stopper or baby food jar

○ Plastic cup
○ 95 percent ethanol
○ Toothpick
○ Shampoo

What You Do

1. Add 2 teaspoons (10 ml) of salt to 4½ cups of water to make a 10 percent salt solution.

2. Mix 1 tablespoon of shampoo with 3 tablespoons of water to make a 25 percent soap solution.

3. Chill the ethanol in the refrigerator until it is needed.

4. Swish about 2 teaspoons of the salt water solution in your mouth for at least 30 seconds. This will remove dead cells (and the DNA they contain) from your cheeks and mouth.

5. Spit out the salt water into a plastic cup.

6. Pour 1 teaspoon (5 ml) of soap solution into the test tube and add the salt water you swished.

7. Seal the test tube and gently rock the solution for 2 minutes. Be careful not to shake the test tube vigorously so you don't break the long strands of DNA into small pieces. (Human cheek cells are more fragile than plant cells.)

8. Open the jar and carefully pour 1 teaspoon (5 ml) of the chilled ethanol down the side of the tube so that it floats on top of the solution containing the DNA.

9. Let the test tube sit still for 1 minute. The DNA will gather in the border between the ethanol and the soapy solution.

10. With a toothpick, carefully pull the DNA out of the test tube and wind it around the toothpick.

Don't swallow!!

Take a Closer Look

In order to take the DNA out of the *cell,* first you must break open the cells. The food processor mushes up the plant and breaks the cell walls. Then the soap in the extraction solution destroys the rest of the cell walls and the membrane of the *nucleus,* letting out the DNA. The salt in the solution causes the proteins and carbohydrates that make up the rest of the cell to sink to the bottom while the DNA stays on top. Cooling the mixture protects the DNA from *enzymes* in the cell that can destroy the DNA. These enzymes are in the cell to protect us from outside DNA, like viruses. Adding cool ethanol to the mixture simply increases the amount of DNA you are able to separate from the rest of the cell parts. Since different plants (and animals, for that matter) have different amounts of DNA, how much you can extract from each plant should vary in the same way.

What is DNA?

DNA stands for *DeoxyriboNucleic Acid.* This long molecule is found in the nucleus of the cells of just about every living thing. Human DNA taken from a single cell is about 6 feet long!

This long molecule is in the shape of a ladder that has been twisted. This shape is called a double helix.

On the ends of each rung of the ladder are smaller molecules called bases. There are only four different bases, but each strand of DNA has millions of bases in all sorts of combinations. This provides all the information needed to make an organism (such as you!) and keep it working.

A single strand of DNA is called a *chromosome.* Different organisms have different numbers of chromosomes (humans have 46). Sections of the chromosomes that determine certain traits (such as eye color or how many toes you have) are called *genes.* These genes actually help make proteins that control how an organism grows and behaves, at least on a cellular level. When an organism reproduces, DNA from the parents is passed on to the child and combined to make a new set of chromosomes. That's why you have some traits from your mom and others from your dad.

DNA Helix

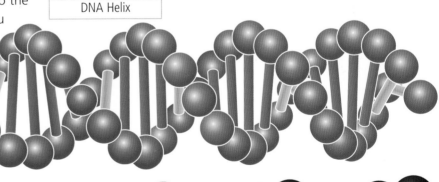

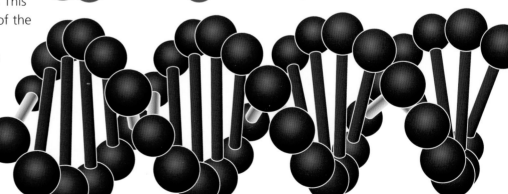

Bones

Forensic anthropologists study bodies long after they are dead. Often, all they have to work with are bones, and usually not a full skeleton. In those cases, the anthropologists rely on clues found in a few bones to reveal the age, gender, race, and even height of the body. The tibia and humerus are two bones whose length may correlate to total height.

Problem

How does the length of your tibia and humerus correspond to your height?

Experiment Summary

You'll measure the length of the tibia and humerus as well as the height of boys and girls of the same age and make a graph to find the relationship between these values.

What You Need

- 10 boys and 10 girls of about the same age
- Metric tape measure
- Graph paper
- Pencil
- Ruler

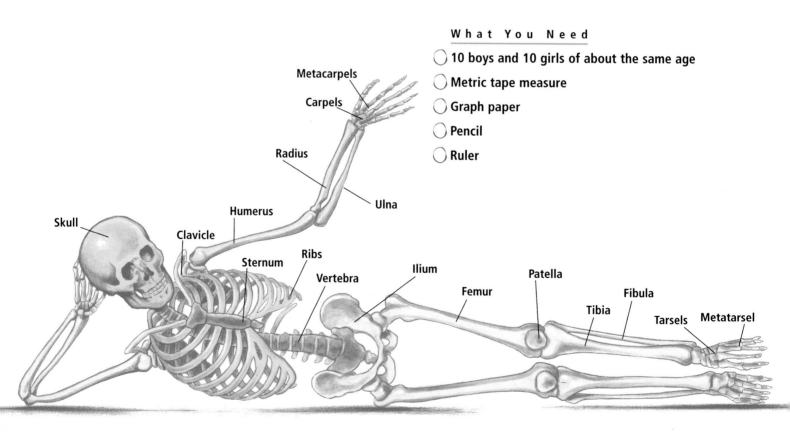

Experimental Procedure

1. For each of your 20 volunteers, carefully measure and record their gender and height in centimeters. Then measure and record the length of each volunteer's humerus and tibia. Practice on yourself first. Make sure you measure both the left- and the right-side bones of each volunteer. Be as careful as possible—you'll need an accurate and precise measurement.

2. For each volunteer, average the measurements for their left and right tibias and left and right humerus.

3. Use the graph paper to make a scatter plot (a graph with just the data points) of your data for tibia length and height for the boys. Remember the independent variable (height) goes on the x-axis and the dependent variable (tibia length) is on the y-axis.

4. Use the ruler to draw a straight line that goes through or close to all of your points. Choose this line carefully and make sure it goes through as many data points as possible. Make the line long enough so that it goes through the y-axis.

5. Calculate the *slope* of your line. Choose two points on your line. Subtract the y values (tibia length) to get the rise of the line, or how high the line goes between these two points. Subtract the x values (height) of these two points to get the run of the line or how far the line goes horizontally between the points. To find the slope, just divide the rise by the run. Write the slope on your graph. Slope describes how much the line slants. (For example, a large slope is a very steep line.)

6. Note where the line crosses the y-axis and write this on your graph. This is called the y-intercept.

7. You can now make an equation that relates the height of a boy to the length of his tibia: Tibia = slope x height + y-intercept

8. Repeat steps 3 to 7 for the tibias of the girls in your group. Then do the same thing with the humerus measurements. Remember to plot the boys' data and the girls' data on separate graphs.

Tips

Finding Your Bones

To measure the humerus, bend your elbow and find the knob on the outside. This knob (or *tuberosity*) is the end of the humerus. There is a similar knob at the other end in the shoulder. Measure from the bottom of the knob in the elbow to the top of the knob in the shoulder.

To measure the tibia, sit in a chair with your legs bent and your shoes and socks off. Find the tuberosity that sticks out on the outside of your ankle. Measure from the bottom of this knob to just below your kneecap.

Explore Further

Compare the bone-to-height relationship for boys and girls of different ages and races. Try measuring different bones such as the femur (the long bone that stretches from the hip socket to the kneecap), head height or other bones you can easily measure. Which are more accurate or consistent in obtaining height from bone length?

Conclusion

How accurate do you think you were at measuring the length of the tibia and humerus? Within how many centimeters do you think you were for the actual length of the bone: 1 cm, 5 cm, or 10 cm? How could you improve the accuracy of your measurements? Which was easier—measuring the tibia or humerus?

How accurate was the line you drew through the points? This is called a line of best fit. Could you make the line fit better? How?

Compare the equations using the tibia lengths for boys and girls. Which had the largest slope? Compare the equations for humerus lengths for boys and girls. Which had the largest slope? Is this what you would expect? What could a tibia's length tell you about the person it belongs to?

FORENSIC CAREERS

Forensic Anthropologist

Do you like biology, history, archeology, and solving puzzles? If you do, you might want to be a forensic anthropologist. Anthropologists study everything that has to do with human beings. Some study modern and ancient cultures, some study how language develops in different parts of the world, and others dig up the ruins of cities. Forensic anthropology is part of what is called *physical anthropology,* or the study of the human body, particularly the bones. Forensic anthropologists deal with the remains of bodies involved in crimes. They help investigators and criminalists figure out who the body is and what happened to it.

What Do Forensic Anthropologists Do?

- Dig up bodies that have been found and preserve as many clues to their identity as possible.
- Determine the age, sex, race, height, and identity of bodies.
- Sometimes they are able figure out how the person died.

How Do They Do It?

It's all in the bones! Below are some of the methods forensic anthropologists use to find out who the bones belong to:

- Match teeth to dental records.
- Analyze the shape of the skull to determine the race of the body.
- Analyze the pelvis to decide if the body is male or female.
- Measure the length of different bones to figure out how tall the body was.
- Figure out how old the body was when it died from the development of the leg bones.
- Extract DNA (if possible) to analyze for information on the identity of the body.
- Perform facial restoration on the skull to make an image of what the person's face looked like.

How Can I Become a Forensic Anthropologist?

You'll need a college degree in chemistry, biology, anatomy, physiology, or anthropology and probably a graduate degree (a doctoral degree is best) in anthropology or human biology. After that, you'll need at least three years of experience in the field before the American Board of Forensic Anthropology can officially certify you. Most forensic anthropologists work at universities or research centers and consult with criminalists and investigators when their help is needed.

The Body Farm

If you ask Dr. Bill Bass where he works, he'll tell you he works on a farm. But this farm doesn't grow corn—it harvests bodies! The Body Farm at the University of Tennessee (officially called the Anthropology Research Facility) was set up by Dr. Bass in 1980 so that forensic anthropologists can study how bodies decay. This helps them figure out exactly when murder victims died. Bodies are scattered about the farm in all sorts of conditions so that the anthropologists can observe them over time. They ask questions like, "How does the temperature of a body change depending on whether it's left in the sunshine or shade?" and "How does a body in a car decompose differently from one in a stream?" After the body has decomposed completely, they collect data from the skeleton to help scientists make predictions of body height and other characteristics. The Body Farm also provides training for the FBI, police groups, and the dogs who help investigators locate bodies.

EyeWitness

When a crime is committed, it's often done in front of somebody. That information seems like it would be really helpful, but what if your eyewitness can't remember, changes his story, or might be lying? How do forensic scientists analyze the evidence collected through eyewitness accounts?

A Timely Observation

You'd think the most useful piece of evidence an investigator can find is an eyewitness. However, in most cases, eyewitness accounts aren't that accurate, particularly if the criminal is a stranger. How well do you think you could identify a criminal if you witnessed a crime in progress?

Problem

How does an eyewitness report vary with time?

Experiment Summary

You'll create a video of a "crime" and see how well your friends describe the criminal immediately after viewing the crime and some time later.

What You Need

- Video camera
- 4 friends
- Brightly colored clothing
- Television
- 20 volunteers
- Surveys

Experimental Procedure

1. With the video camera and four friends, create a short video of a simple "crime." For example, you could film a couple of friends playing catch and a "criminal" could come along and take the ball. Your "criminal" should be on screen for only 10 seconds or less and have a couple of bright-colored items on, such as a jacket or hat. Make sure that the person you choose to play the criminal isn't someone the rest of your volunteers know.

2. Create a list of 10 to 15 questions about your video. Some questions you may want to include are:

- Describe what happened in the movie.
- Was the person who stole the ball male or female?
- Was the person who stole the ball wearing a hat?
- Describe what the person who stole the ball was wearing.
- How old do you think the person who stole the ball is?
- How tall do you think the person who stole the ball is?

3. Gather your volunteers. Show them the movie. Do not tell your volunteers what the movie is about or that you'll be asking them questions about it afterward. (Just tell them it's your science fair experiment!)

4. Give half the group the survey immediately after they see the movie.

5. Have the entire group complete the same survey 24 hours later.

Conclusion

Compile the results of your survey. Calculate the percentage of correct answers for the group that completed the survey right after they watched the movie. Then calculate the percentage of their correct answers the second time they took the quiz. Calculate the percentage of correct answers for the group that only took the test after 24 hours had passed. Which group most accurately observed the crime, the group that completed the survey immediately after watching the video or the group that waited until the next day? Did the first group change their answers at all when completing the survey the second time? Were there questions that no one got right? Any questions that everyone got right?

Explore Further

Investigate the power of suggestion. Tell some of the viewers what they'll see before viewing the movie (friends playing catch, or even someone stealing a ball). How does this affect their eyewitness accounts? Create other movies where the criminal appears for different lengths of time, in different light levels, or at different distances, and see how this affects your results. Create mug shots of your criminal along with the other actors and other people not involved in your project. See if the volunteers can pick out the criminal.

Take a Closer Look

While witnesses might not intentionally mislead an investigator, their memories may not be exactly accurate. Memory can be divided into three stages: *encoding, storage,* and *retrieval.* There are many opportunities for problems to occur in creating and reporting memories of an event such as a crime. The first stage, encoding, describes how what the witness sees, hears, and feels combines to make the memory. Stress causes this information to be lost or encoded incorrectly and can alter their perception of what actually happened. Witnessing a crime certainly causes stress!

Interference and *decay* can both reduce the accuracy of stored information. Interference can occur when the eyewitness is asked misleading questions after the crime, which get in the way of information that he stored during the crime. For example, if an investigator asks, "Was the car red?" the witness might think he remembers a red car. Instead, the question should be, "What color was the car?" Decay is the weakening of memories as time passes. It's best to ask questions of the witnesses as soon as possible after a crime so that the memories are still fresh.

Did You See What I Saw?

Back in the nineteenth century and earlier, eyewitness testimony was the only evidence accepted in court. These days, lawyers, judges, and juries recognize that memory is highly subjective and eyewitnesses to the same crime can give very different reports. For example, consider the case of a woman who was attacked in her own front yard. Three neighbors and a passerby who called the police witnessed the crime. Here are the descriptions of one of the attackers they gave the police:

Neighbor 1: "tall, black, with bleached blonde hair"

Neighbor 2: "tall, Hispanic, with a light-colored ski-type hat"

Neighbor 3: "medium height, medium complexion, and medium brown hair"

Passerby at the phone booth: "average height, white, and some sort of colored tints in his hair, like blue or green or something on the tips"

All of the witnesses agreed that the attacker was a young man. Police finally apprehended the criminal: a tall woman of Hispanic background with auburn hair!

Obviously, the witnesses were not reliable in this case. However, the crime took place at dusk, and the low light, combined with the artificial light of the street lamps, altered how the witnesses saw the attacker. Investigators had a hard time accounting for the blue or green-colored hair described by the passerby until they visited the phone booth and saw that the tinted glass would cause the woman's highlighted hair to appear bluish.

Lie Detection

Physical evidence may be difficult to analyze, but it doesn't lie. People, on the other hand, often do lie, especially if they are accused of a crime. Investigators need to be able to tell if a suspect or witness is telling the truth. A lie detector, a machine that measures your blood pressure, pulse, and other indicators of stress to show if you're telling the truth, is used in some cases. Most of the time investigators need to rely on body language (how suspects move or gesture) to figure out if the person they are interviewing is trying to mislead them.

Problem

How is a person's body language affected by whether she's lying or not?

Experiment Summary

You'll interview volunteers and record their *body language* to try to determine who is lying and who is telling the truth.

What You Need

- Pen
- Note cards
- 10 or more volunteers
- Paper
- Video camera (optional)

Experimental Procedure

1. Label half of the note cards "Truth" and the other half "Lie." You should have as many note cards as volunteers.

2. Have each of your volunteers select a card so that you don't know who will be lying and who will be telling the truth. Explain to the volunteers that you'll be interviewing them. If their card says "Truth," they should only tell the truth, and if their card says "Lie," then they should make up answers to the questions. Encourage them to make up answers that are believable. (If a volunteer says he had lunch with the Queen of England on Saturday, you'll know he was lying.)

3. Make a table to record your data. Across the top of the page, make five columns: "Touches Face or Head," "Avoids Eye Contact," "Says Umm" (or similar sound), "Fidgets with Hands," and "Other Observations." Make a row for each person you interview.

4. Interview each of the volunteers individually. Ask them to describe what they did last Saturday (or some other day, if you already know what they did last Saturday). Ask questions to encourage your volunteers to provide detail. For example, if a volunteer says he had lunch, ask him what he had for lunch and where he ate.

5. During the interview, make a mark in the column for each of the volunteer's actions. For example, if he scratches his head, make a mark under "Touches Face or Head." If you observe anything else interesting, be sure to write it down under "Other Observations." You may wish to set up a video camera to record the volunteer during the interview so you can check your data again later.

6. After each of the interviews, write down whether you think the volunteer is telling the truth or lying. Then ask the volunteers to return their cards so that you know if your suspicions are correct.

7. Repeat steps 4 through 6 for each of the volunteers.

8. For each volunteer, add up the number of marks in each column. Average the number of marks in each column for the liars and the truth-tellers.

Conclusion

Make a bar graph of the average number of marks for each of the actions you recorded for the liars and another for the truth-tellers. Are there any big differences in the number of times members of each group did certain actions? That is, did liars avoid eye contact more, or did truth-tellers fidget with their hands more? You can figure out how likely a liar is to do a certain action by calculating a *ratio*. Divide the number of times the liars avoided eye contact by the number of times the truth-tellers avoided eye contact. This number tells you how much more often liars avoided eye contact than truth-tellers. For example, if the liars avoided eye contact an average of 12 times and truth-tellers avoided eye contact an average of three times, the ratio is 12:3 or 4. That is, liars avoid eye contact four times more often than truth-tellers.

Were you able to tell who was lying and who was telling the truth before you analyzed your data? What about after you analyzed your data?

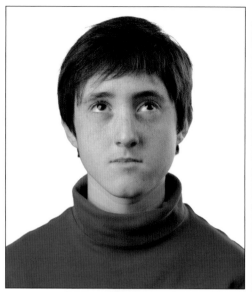

Would you trust this face?

Explore Further

What other signs could you look for to tell if someone is lying? Share your findings with your volunteers and repeat the experiment to see if the liars can change their body language.

Polygraphs

Occasionally, a judge or lawyer may ask a suspect or witness to submit to a *polygraph* or lie detector test. A polygraph is a machine that records data from different body systems such as respiration (breathing), blood pressure, and sweat glands while a subject (the person being examined) is answering questions. The polygraph examiner compares the subject's reactions when they are known to be telling the truth or lying to their reactions on the questions investigators need the answers to.

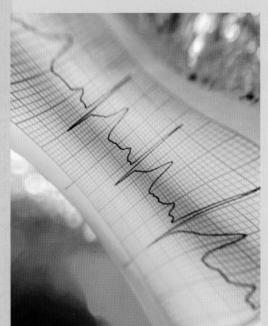

A polygraph machine uses tubes connected to the chest to measure how the subject breathes. Two small metal plates attached to the fingers measure how the person sweats and a cuff around the arm measures blood pressure. These devices are connected to needles or pens that record the measurements on a piece of paper. The graph that is produced is called a polygraph chart.

In the movies and on television, the needles are shown moving wildly and the polygraph examiner announces that the subject is lying. In real life, this isn't necessarily the case.

When a polygraph is given, the examiner first asks the subject questions and they answer truthfully. For example, "What is your name?" or "What day is it?" Next, they ask the subject to lie on purpose so they can see what their reaction is when they lie. The examiner will then ask the questions relevant to the case or crime committed and compare the measurements taken to the subject's answers when they were telling the truth and lying. There are three possible results for any question. The subject may be telling the truth, lying, or the results may be inconclusive. That is, the examiner might be unable to tell if the subject is telling the truth or not. Some physical factors such as drug and alcohol use or even hunger can mislead a polygraph machine. Simple tricks, like self-inflicted pain by biting the tongue, can confuse the results as well.

New ways of measuring how truthful someone is are being developed all the time. Some machines measure brain activity and others analyze voice patterns. However, even polygraphs are still not widely accepted in the courts because they aren't 100 percent accurate. In fact most polygraph examiners are only right about 85 percent of the time.

Fingers & Feet

Whenever you touch something, your finger leave a mark—no matter how clean your hands are. Wherever you walk, run, jump, or stand, your feet leave an impression. Forensic scientists can collect and analyze this information. Then they'll know where you were, when you were there, and what you were doing.

Lifting Prints

As much as they try, criminals have a hard time keeping their fingerprints off objects at the crime scene. As a forensic scientist, your job is to find the prints and make them visible so you can analyze them. This process is called lifting the print and can be done several different ways.

Problem

How does the method you use to lift a fingerprint affect the quality of the lifted print?

Experiment Summary

You'll make a *fingerprint* on different surfaces and then lift the prints by dusting and exposing them to chemicals.

What You Need

- **Fingerprint testing materials:** aluminum foil, paper, cardboard, cloth, plastic (cut a piece off a plastic drink bottle), wood (break a popsicle stick in two pieces), glass jar
- **Your finger**
- **2 brand-new, soft makeup brushes**
- **Talcum powder**
- **Cocoa powder**
- **Clear tape**
- **White paper**
- **Black paper**
- **Wide-mouth jar with lid (spaghetti or pickle jars work well)**
- **Bottle cap**
- **Super glue***
- **Nail polish remover**
- **Camera**

*Make sure the glue contains cyanoacrylate.

Experimental Procedure

1. Cut, tear, or break the fingerprint testing materials so that you have two pieces of each material. Set one complete set of testing materials aside.

2. Wipe your finger along the side of your nose or through your hair to make it oily. (This will make a clear print.) Apply your finger firmly to each of the testing materials. Get your finger oily before making each print. Be careful not to smear them when handling the objects.

3. To dust for fingerprints, dip a brush into the powder so its bristles are completely coated. If the fingerprint is on a dark-colored object, use the talcum powder. If it's on a light-colored object, use the cocoa powder.

4. Gently brush back and forth across the print so that the powder sticks to the fingerprint. Sweep away any extra powder.

5. Take a piece of clear tape and carefully and firmly lay it down over the fingerprint so there aren't any air bubbles. Pull the tape up and stick it on a contrasting piece of paper. (For example, if you used the white talc powder, put the tape on black paper.)

6. Repeat steps 3 through 5 to lift a print from each object you touched.

7. To chemically lift prints, first wash and dry the jar and lid. Then repeat step 2 with the second set of fingerprint testing materials. Put a fingerprint inside the jar so you can use glass as one of your materials. Be careful not to smear the prints.

8. Lay the jar on its side and gently place each object in the jar. Make sure each print is facing upwards and isn't covered by another object. If all of the objects won't fit in the jar, split them into two batches.

9. Carefully squirt just enough glue into the bottle cap so that it covers the bottom of the cap. Don't get any on your fingers! (If you do, soak your finger in fingernail polish remover to get the glue off before continuing the experiment.) Place the bottle cap in the jar with the objects and put the lid on tightly. Let the jar sit in a warm place for one hour.

10. Take the jar outside and remove the lid so the glue fumes can escape. Be careful not to tip the jar—you don't want the objects and glue falling on each other.

11. Remove each of the objects and observe the fingerprints. Record what you see in your notebook and take photos of each print. Compare them to the prints you got from dusting. You may wish to repeat the experiment a couple more times to make sure your results are consistent.

Conclusion

Compare the prints obtained from both methods on each material. Which materials revealed the fingerprints better by dusting and which by chemical lifting? Is there any similarity between the objects that worked best for each method? Did any of the materials not show fingerprints by either method? (If so, repeat the experiment for this material just to be sure.) Which method was easiest to perform? Which method was best for visualizing the fingerprints? Which method do you think would be best to use at a crime scene? Can you think of any disadvantages to using either method?

Explore Further

Try these methods on other materials. If they won't fit in the jar, you can use a large cardboard box, or any other container you can seal. Try other ways of lifting fingerprints. Instead of super glue, you can use iodine crystals. (Ask your science teacher where you can get some.) Experiment with different powders for dusting the prints.

Take a Closer Look

When you *dust for fingerprints,* the powder sticks to the oils and sweat left by the ridges of your finger so that you can see the print pattern. However, if you're not careful, you can smear the fingerprint in the process. To avoid this, do not touch the bristles on the brush since you'll leave oils and sweat on the brush, which could interfere with the print you're trying to dust. You also want to be very careful not to push down or rub the tape when lifting the dusted fingerprint or attaching it to the paper.

The chemical method with super glue that you used to visualize the fingerprints is also known as the *cyanoacrylate fuming method.* (Cyanoacrylate is a chemical found in super glue.) This method was first used in Japan in 1978 and is now used widely around the world because it's cheap, easy, and reliable—and not as messy as dusting!

The chemicals in the glue evaporate into the air when the air inside the jar heats up. When the glue fumes come in contact with the sweat and oil that makes up the fingerprint, they react to form a white material that you can see. If you let this print sit out in the air after being fumed with super glue, it will get hard and can be photographed or easily transported to a forensic laboratory. To speed up the process, some criminalists will heat the container with the glue and fingerprints so that the chemicals evaporate into the air faster.

Family Fingerprints

Look closely at your fingertips. The network of ridges and valleys make a distinct pattern. There is no way to alter this pattern, and it's nearly impossible to touch anything without leaving a fingerprint. For these reasons, fingerprints are one of the most powerful pieces of evidence crime scene investigators have for identifying criminals.

Problem

How do your genes determine your fingerprint patterns?

Experiment Summary

You'll compare the fingerprints of children to the fingerprints of their parents to see if they have common characteristics.

What You Need

◯ Black inkpad or fingerprint kit

◯ Index cards

◯ 4 families (parents and their children)

◯ Magnifying glass

◯ Hand wipes

◯ Fingerprint chart (see page 53)

Experimental Procedure

1. Press your finger against the inkpad, evenly coating the area from your nail to the first knuckle of your finger with ink. Gently place your finger on an index card. (The weight of your finger provides enough pressure to make the print. Pressing down will blur the print.) If your print is too light, you need more ink on your finger. If it's too dark and you can't see the details, you need less ink on your finger. Practice taking your own fingerprints until your prints are clear.

2. Before you begin to collect fingerprints, have your volunteer wash and dry his hands thoroughly. (Dirt and oils will mess up the prints.) Label an index card with the volunteer's name. On the index card, carefully make a print of each of the fingers on his right hand. Don't forget the thumb.

3. Repeat step 2 with each volunteer.

4. Categorize the main characteristics of each print using the fingerprint chart. Identify the primary trait of each finger and write it next to the print. For example, if you identify a radial loop on the thumb, then write "radial loop" below the thumbprint; if you identify a mound on the index finger, write "mound" below the index fingerprint. Analyze each of the cards this way. If you notice other common characteristics, note them on the card as well.

Family Similarity Chart

Index Finger	Parent 1	Parent 2	Kid 1	Kid 2
Whorl				
Arch	X			X
Loop		X	X	

5. For each family, make a chart for each finger to see if there are any common characteristics.

Conclusion

How many fingerprints from children matched one or more of their parents'? What percentage of the fingerprints is this? Make a pie graph to show how many children matched their mother's fingerprints, father's fingerprints, or had no match at all. What does this tell you about the link between genetics and fingerprints?

Which were the most common fingerprint patterns? Did you find any unusual fingerprints?

Explore Further

Can you take toe prints or footprints instead of fingerprints? Do they have similar patterns and are they inherited? Use food coloring to take nose prints from cats and dogs. What types of patterns do you see? Are the nose prints of animals from the same breed more or less similar than the nose prints of different breeds?

Debbie

Susan

Dad

Mom

Mike

Take A Closer Look

The skin on the palms of your hands and soles of your feet contains more sweat glands than any other part of your body. You may also notice a pattern of ridges and furrows that makes up your handprints and footprints. This skin is called *friction ridge skin*. The furrows are like channels that funnel the sweat off the surface of your hand so you can hold onto whatever you grab—kind of like the tread on a tire.

Your fingerprints are formed long before you're born. Genetics is a big factor in what your fingerprints look like, but environmental factors, such as the kind of nutrition your mother gets while you're developing in her womb, also affect the pattern. In fact, identical twins, with identical DNA, will have different fingerprints. The large patterns (whorls, arches, and loops) will be the same, but differences in the individual ridge features make it possible to tell them apart.

Your fingerprint pattern doesn't change as you get older. The ridges usually get bigger, but the pattern stays the same. There may even be a correlation between the width of the fingerprint ridges and your height.

Some people have attempted to destroy their fingerprints by burning, cutting, or even plastic surgery, with no success. The only thing that can really alter a fingerprint is a scar. Because of this, criminals often wear gloves or try to wipe off everything they touch. However, you can't usually see fingerprints, so some prints are nearly always left behind.

Fingerprints & Forensics

There are three types of fingerprints that can be found at a crime scene.

Plastic or molded prints are 3-dimensional fingerprints that occur when fingerprints are left in a soft substance like soap or clay and are not very common.

Visible prints can be found when ink, blood, or some other substance is on the fingers so that the print is easily seen. These aren't very common either.

Latent prints are the most common type of fingerprint. Latent prints occur when the sweat on your hands and fingers leaves an invisible imprint on whatever you touch. Since they can't be seen with the naked eye, investigators use special techniques to see them (see page 49). Recently, researchers discovered that sweat glows when illuminated with certain types of lasers. Photographs can then be taken of the glowing fingerprints. This method is expensive, so most investigators use the powder method.

Originally, fingerprints were kept on note cards like the ones you made in this experiment and investigators had to organize them in file cabinets. Now all fingerprints are kept on computers in an automated fingerprint identification system (AFIS) that automatically classifies and stores fingerprints that are scanned in digitally. This makes it easier for investigators all over the world to discover the identity of criminals.

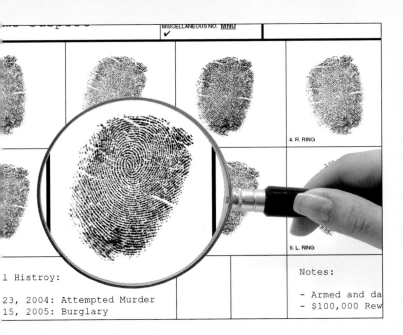

Fingerprint History

Ancient Chinese and Babylonian civilizations used finger-prints to sign legal documents, and some artists still use their fingerprints to sign their work. But it wasn't until the 1880s that fingerprints were used to identify individuals.

Around 1880, William Herschel, a British administrator in Bengal, started using handprints on contracts because workers would change their signatures to get out of doing work. At the same time, Dr. Henry Faulds, a British doctor working in Tokyo, suggested using fingerprints for identification. Sir Francis Galton, a cousin of Charles Darwin, jumped on Dr. Faulds' idea (and stole all the credit) and performed experiments to see if fingerprints changed and if any two people could have the same fin-gerprint. His results showed that fingerprints were ideal for identifying people. And in 1897, Sir Edward Henry, an Indian police officer, came up with the classification sys-tem for fingerprints that we use today.

While all of this was going on, Europe was having a huge crime problem. The courts wanted to be able to punish repeat offenders more harshly than first timers. The crimi-nals could fool the system by giving a different name each time they were arrested. France and England in particular were desperate for a way to identify their criminals and first jumped on *anthropometrics* (see Try This!), or body measurements such as arm length or head width, as a solution. While trained scientists had no trouble taking accurate measurements, the policeman on the street was not so careful and the system was doomed. It wasn't long before they realized that fingerprints were easier to take and analyze. By 1901, fingerprints were used all over the world to identify criminals.

However, it was quite a jump from identifying a person you have already arrested to using fingerprints to solve a crime when your suspect is long gone. For several years, the courts and juries likened fingerprints to palm reading and refused to send someone to jail, or even worse, the death sentence, based on a fingerprint. But by 1905 in London, fingerprint evidence was responsible for the con-viction of the Stratton brothers for the murder of paint store owners Thomas and Ann Farrow, and soon such evidence was accepted in courtrooms everywhere. It's hard to believe that the most common piece of evidence collected at modern crime scenes was never even consid-ered just over a century ago!

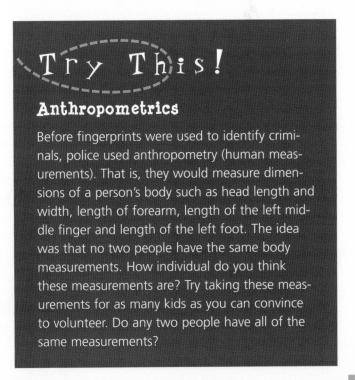

Try This!

Anthropometrics

Before fingerprints were used to identify crimi-nals, police used anthropometry (human meas-urements). That is, they would measure dimen-sions of a person's body such as head length and width, length of forearm, length of the left mid-dle finger and length of the left foot. The idea was that no two people have the same body measurements. How individual do you think these measurements are? Try taking these meas-urements for as many kids as you can convince to volunteer. Do any two people have all of the same measurements?

Footprints

A series of footprints can tell criminalists a lot about what the criminal looks like and what happened at a crime scene. From a few footprints you can deduce the approximate height, weight, and walking pattern of a person, as well as whether she was walking, running, or even carrying a heavy object.

Problem

How does height affect stride?

Experiment Summary

You'll measure the stride of several people of different heights and make a graph to determine if stride and height are related.

What You Need

- ○ Flour
- ○ Meter stick or yard stick
- ○ 20 volunteers of different heights
- ○ Stopwatch
- ○ Broom

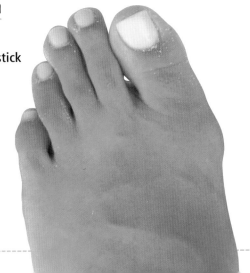
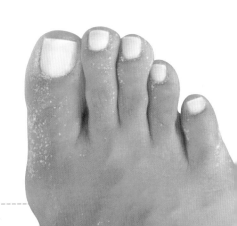

Experimental Procedure

1. Find a flat space where you can make a mess with flour. Sprinkle the flour in an area about 2 feet (0.6 meters) wide and 12 feet (3.7 meters) long.

2. Draw a start line and a finish line in the flour with your finger. Carefully measure the distance between these two lines. You'll use this distance to calculate the average walking speed of your volunteers.

3. Use the meter stick or yardstick to measure the height of your first volunteer with her shoes on. Record her height.

4. Ask the volunteer to walk normally on the flour so that she leaves at least three or four footprints along the length of the floured area. While she's walking, use the stopwatch to time how long it takes her to walk between the start and finish lines. Record the time it takes.

5. Calculate and record the average walking speed of the volunteer by dividing the distance between the start and finish lines by the time it took her to walk the distance.

6. Carefully measure and record the distance between the prints from the toe of one foot to the heel of the next. Calculate the average distance between the prints.

7. Use the broom to sweep over the footprints. Sprinkle more flour on the floor if you need to cover up any blank spots.

8. Repeat steps 3 to 7 for each of your volunteers.

Conclusion

Make a line graph of height versus the average distance between footprints for all your volunteers. (Each volunteer will be a data point on the graph.) Is there a relationship between these two variables? How does the distance between footprints change as height increases? Make another line graph of height versus average walking speed. (Again, each volunteer will be a data point on the graph.) How does walking speed change with height? Could you predict the height of a suspect based on their footprints? Try it out with some new volunteers, measuring their stride first and then guess at their height. Measure their height and see how close you got.

Explore Further

In this experiment, your volunteers or "suspects" walked at a normal pace on a flat, hard surface. How would other variables affect the relationship between footprints and height? Have your volunteers walk on different surfaces such as sand, mud, or hilly terrain. What if they walked barefoot? Load up a backpack with heavy books and see if carrying a heavy load affects the distance between prints. Have the volunteers wear the backpack on just one shoulder, and see if you can tell from the footprints which side the backpack was on.

What other characteristics of a suspect can be found from her footprints? Compare leg length and weight to the distance between footprints.

Take a look at the footprints themselves. Do different parts of the foot, like the toe, heel, or instep leave different prints when the volunteers vary their speed? What if they run, skip, or hop? Could you tell how someone was moving based on her footprint?

Take a Closer Look

When looking at footprints, there are seven basic types of measurements referred to as gait patterns. The first is the stride from one foot to another as described in this experiment. A short stride suggests the suspect was carrying something, but a long stride indicates that the suspect was running.

Measuring the distance from the toe of one foot to the heel of the same foot may indicate if the suspect has a limp. The distribution of weight on the foot can also be determined from a footprint. That is, does the footprint suggest that a suspect put her heel or toe down first in a step?

The length and depth of a footprint can give clues to the approximate size of the suspect. For example, a short, light person will leave a short, shallow print, but a tall, heavy person will leave a large, deep print.

Criminalists also measure the angle at which the toe points away from the direction of motion, the width between the steps (the space between the inside of the right foot and the inside of the left foot), as well as the general distribution of the prints to determine if the crime was planned out or more random.

Sherlock Holmes

The following is an excerpt from "A Study in Scarlet" by Sir Arthur Conan Doyle, in which Dr. Watson describes the first case he witnessed Sherlock Holmes solve. Here Sherlock Holmes describes how he determined that the suspect must be about 6 feet tall.

"Why, the height of a man, in nine cases out of ten, can be told from the length of his stride. It is a simple calculation enough, though there is no use my boring you with figures. I had this fellow's stride both on the clay outside and on the dust within. Then I had a way of checking my calculation. When a man writes on a wall, his instinct leads him to write above the level of his own eyes. Now, that writing was just over six feet from the ground. It was child's play."

Later, Sherlock Holmes shares more clues that have been revealed by the footprints.

"I'll tell you one other thing," he said. "Patent-leathers and Square-toes came in the same cab, and they walked down the pathway together as friendly as possible— arm-in-arm, in all probability. When they got inside, they walked up and down the room- or rather—Patent-leathers stood still while Square-toes walked up and down. I could read all that in the dust; and I could read that as he walked he grew more and more excited. That is shown by the increased length of his strides. He was talking all the while, and working himself up, no doubt, into a fury. Then the tragedy occurred. I've told you all I know myself now, for the rest is mere surmise and conjecture."

Upon solving the case, Sherlock Holmes proclaims, "There is no branch of detective science which is so important and so much neglected as the art of tracing footsteps."

Casting Prints

Just about anything can cause a print: fingers, hands, feet, shoes, tires, tools, and even ears. (These are sometime used to catch a robber who puts his ear up to a safe to crack the lock's combination.) Often criminals try to avoid leaving prints by wearing gloves or wiping off surfaces they touch, but they usually forget about the prints caused by their feet or shoes. Sometimes forensic scientists are fortunate enough to find these prints in a soft surface like soil, snow, or sand, so that the print is actually three-dimensional. In this case, a cast can be poured in the print so that a three-dimensional model can be taken back to the lab for analysis or compared directly to a suspect's shoe.

Problem

How does the casting method affect the accuracy and durability of the cast?

Experiment Summary

You'll pour casts of shoeprints using dental stone and plaster of Paris to see which gives the most accurate and durable print.

What You Need

- ◯ Cardboard
- ◯ Scissors
- ◯ Tape
- ◯ Petroleum jelly
- ◯ Broom or shovel
- ◯ Sandbox
- ◯ Water
- ◯ Shoes
- ◯ Large paper cups
- ◯ Plaster of Paris*
- ◯ Water

- ◯ 4 paint stirring sticks
- ◯ Straw
- ◯ 2 pounds of dental stone (available from dental supply stores)*
- ◯ Stopwatch

Do not pour plaster of Paris or dental stone down the sink as it can clog the pipes. Always mix your casting materials in paper cups or other disposable containers.

Experimental Procedure

1. Cut 2-inch strips of cardboard and tape them together to make a 6-inch by 12-inch rectangular frame.

2. Coat the inside of your frame with petroleum jelly. (This will keep the cast from sticking to your frame so you can reuse the frame.)

3. Use a broom or shovel to smooth out and level a 2-foot by 2-foot area in the sandbox. Gently sprinkle water over the sand until it's slightly damp. Do not make any puddles.

4. Carefully put one foot in the damp, smoothed out area. Put all of your weight on that foot, then remove it very carefully so as not to mess up your clean shoeprint.

Tips

If you have trouble making prints because the sand is too fine, try using a light dusting of talcum powder or hair spray to stabilize the impression before pouring the cast. If you use hair spray, do not spray it directly on the print, just spray it in the air and let the cloud settle on the ground.

5. Place the frame around your shoe print.

6. Follow the manufacturer's instructions to mix the plaster of Paris and water together in the paper cup. Use the paint stirring stick to mix the plaster.

7. Slowly pour the plaster over the shoeprint so that it is about 1 inch deep, and allow it to dry for one hour.

8. Gently remove the cast from the sand box and cardboard frame and bring it indoors. Allow the cast to dry overnight before brushing off any sand that may have stuck to your cast.

9. Repeat steps 2 through 8, but this time add ¼ cup of straw to every cup of plaster mixture. The straw will help stabilize the plaster cast.

10. Repeat steps 2 through 5 again, using the dental stone to make the cast.

11. Follow the instructions on the package to mix the dental stone. You will need about 2½ pounds of dental stone for one cast. Let the cast dry for 30 minutes before removing it, and then allow it to dry another 24 hours before cleaning off any sand that may have stuck to the cast.

Conclusion

Carefully inspect the bottom of each cast. Which is the most accurate, that is, which provides the most detail for identifying a possible match to the shoeprint? Did any of the casts break apart or experience chipping during the experiment? Which of the recipes produced the most fragile cast and which produced the most durable cast? Which recipe would you recommend be used to collect shoeprint data at crime scenes? You may also want to take into account ease of use, time to set, and cost in your decision.

Plaster of Paris and dental stone are names for calcium sulfate hemihydrate (one molecule of water for every two molecules of calcium sulfate), which reacts with water to form gypsum, or calcium sulfate dihydrate (two molecules of water for each molecule of calcium sulfate). During this reaction, heat is released. (See if you can feel the temperature of the plaster rise as you mix in the water.) While the chemistry of plaster of Paris and dental stone is the same, the finer and purer powder of dental stone creates a more regular crystal that sets faster and provides more detail in the casts.

Matching a shoeprint to the shoe that made it is done in two steps. First, forensic scientists see if the print and shoe belong to the same class. That is, are they both the same model of running shoe, or are they different brands of sandals? If they match, investigators look for matching *accidental characteristics*. Accidental characteristics are cuts, wear patterns, or other marks that make the shoe unique. Some cuts or marks are created in the manufacturing process, and wear patterns are caused by the size of a person's foot and the way he walks.

Shoeprints can also be useful for providing links to previous crimes. For example, a thief in England robbed a sporting goods store and stole a new pair of shoes in the process. Days later, the staff found the old shoes he had left in the box at the store. The police were able to match his old shoes to prints he had left while committing a crime for which he had previously been arrested. With this information, the police were able to locate the thief and the stolen merchandise.

Explore Further

Adjust the ratios of water to plaster of Paris or dental stone to see if you can make a more accurate, faster-setting print. What other materials can you add to the plaster of Paris to make it more stable? Try grass clippings, toothpicks, or even a wire mesh set over the shoeprint before pouring the plaster.

Try making casts of shoeprints in other materials besides sand, such as soil, mud, or even snow. What's the smallest print you can cast? What's the largest print?

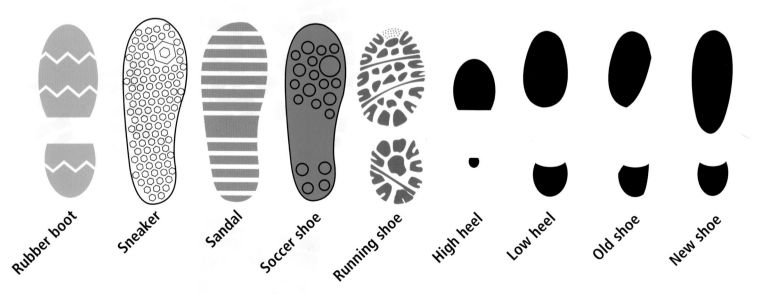

Rubber boot   Sneaker   Sandal   Soccer shoe   Running shoe   High heel   Low heel   Old shoe   New shoe

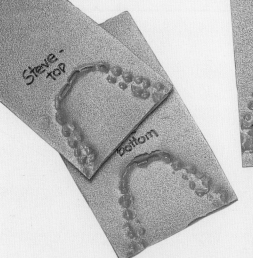

Try This!

Teeth Imprints

Like fingerprints and shoeprints, teeth imprints can also be used to identify criminals. Collect teeth imprints from you and your friends to see if you can find differences in the impressions.

What You Need

○ **Styrofoam plate***

○ **Scissors**

○ **Volunteers**

*Ask for these from the meat department in a grocery store.

What You Do

1. Cut two 4-inch by 3-inch rectangles from the styrofoam plate.

2. Stack two rectangles together and place the narrow end in your mouth as far as you can. (If you gag yourself, you've gone too far.)

3. Bite down firmly on the styrofoam. Label the plates so you know which one has marks from your top teeth and which has marks from your bottom teeth.

4. Repeat steps 1 through 3 on as many volunteers as you can find.

5. When comparing teeth imprints, think about how many teeth made the impressions and which features are the most useful for telling the imprints apart.

The Written Record

Criminals often write things down: ransom notes, instructions, and more. Some criminals specialize in creating forgeries and falsifying documents. This chapter helps you discover how forensic scientists analyze written documents.

Chromatography

What do check forgers, kidnappers, and bank robbers all have in common? They usually leave some sort of writing behind as evidence. Luckily, forensic scientists can analyze the ink in the writing samples using chromatography to help lead police to the bad guys. Write your name with several different pens and compare the ink in the writing samples. Can you tell them apart?

Problem

How do different solvents separate the ink components of ballpoint pens?

Experiment Summary

You'll compare *chromatographs* using alcohol, water, vinegar, and ammonia as solvents to separate the components of pen ink.

What You Need

- Coffee filters
- Scissors
- 4 pencils
- 4 clear, large glasses
- Masking tape
- Ruler
- 3 ballpoint pens that are the same color but different brands
- Isopropyl alcohol
- Vinegar
- Ammonia
- Water
- Ultraviolet lamp (optional)
- Calculator (optional)

1. Cut the coffee filter into four strips. Each strip should be at least 2 inches (5 cm) wide.

2. Wrap one end of each of the coffee filter strips around each pencil, letting the other end dangle. Tape the strip in place so when the pencil rests across the top of the glass, the strip hangs into the glass without touching the sides or bottom.

3. Draw a line across the strip exactly ½ inch (1.3 cm) up from the bottom with a pencil.

4. Using the three different pens, make a pea-sized dot of ink on the line you drew on the bottom of the strip. Make one dot with each type of ink on each strip. Space the dots about ½ inch apart. Use the pencil to label which dot came from which pen below each dot.

5. Label the glasses with the masking tape. Write the type of solvent (alcohol, vinegar, ammonia, or water) you'll be using in each glass on the tape. Label the filter strips in pencil with the type of solvent as well.

6. Remove the filter strips from the glasses. Pour a small amount of solvent into each glass, just filling the bottom.

7. Re-place the pencils across the tops of the glasses so that the bottom of the filter strip touches the solvent but the ink dot doesn't. You may need to adjust the amount of solvent in the glass. Take the filter strip out of the glass before you do this. (If you splash solvent directly on the ink, you'll have to redo the experiment!)

8. Wait 25 to 30 minutes, then remove the filter strips from the solvents. Watch your experiment closely. If the solvent spreads up the filter strip through the ink dot and reaches the pencil before the time is up, take the filter strip out.

9. With the pencil, trace the solvent front, that is, the top edge of the solvent across the top of the strip. Take the strips off the pencils and lay them flat to dry.

10. Once they're dry, inspect the strips carefully. You'll see spots or smears of color between the original ink mark and the solvent front. These spots or smears are the separated components (ingredients) of the ink. If you can see the spots clearly, outline them with a pencil. If the spots are not obvious, try holding the paper under an ultraviolet lamp. (Be careful not to look directly into the lamp!) Some compounds can be seen better this way. Outline each of the spots with a pencil.

11. Now you're ready to calculate the R_f value for each of the separated components of the ink. To do this, measure the distance from the start (the line you drew in pencil at the bottom) to the center of each separated ink spot. Divide this by the total distance from the start line to the solvent front to get the R_f value.

R_f = (distance from the start line to spot center)
        (distance from the start line to solvent front)

Conclusion

R_f stands for "ratio of fronts." The R_f will be the same for a substance or component of the ink that's analyzed in the same way (with the same solvent and filter paper). That means R_f values for known substances can be compared to those of unknown substances so that they can be identified. Did any of the inks contain substances with the same or similar R_f values? Different pens can have some of the same components or ingredients in their inks, so they may have some R_f values in common.

How many different spots did each of the inks produce? The purity of a sample can be seen on the chromatograph. An impure sample will often give two or more spots, while a pure sample will show only one spot.

Compare the solvents used to create each of the chromatographs. Which solvents separated the substances in each of the inks best? Did each of the inks produce the same pattern? Did any of the inks not separate out using any of these solvents? Which solvent took the longest and which took the shortest time to complete?

Take a Closer Look

Chromatography is used by scientists in many fields to break down mixtures of any type into their primary elements, identified by the color separations that result on the paper. These chemical elements are made up of molecules that have different degrees of affinity or attraction to the solvents, which in this experiment included water, alcohol, vinegar, and ammonia. For example, those molecules that have a strong affinity for water (called *hydrophilic*) will cling to the water molecules as they spread out and move up the filter paper. Some molecules are not soluble in water (called *hydrophobic*) and respond better to other solvents like alcohol.

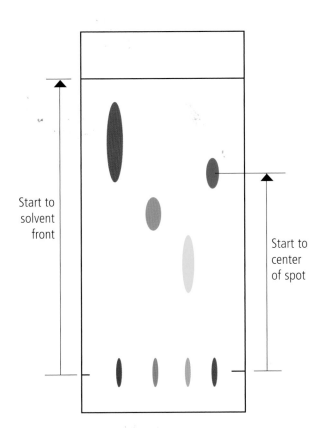

Start to solvent front

Start to center of spot

Other factors also affect the distance the components of the ink travel up the paper:

The composition of the ink. Different companies use different dyes to make their ink. Some try to produce special effects so they cannot be accused of copying another company's ink.

How well each substance in the ink dissolves in the solvent. If the ink does not dissolve in the solvent, it cannot be carried up the paper. This is the case with permanent ink and water. Since the permanent ink is not soluble in water (that's what makes it permanent) the mark stays in the starting place. However, some permanent inks dissolve in other substances, like alcohol (try it out!). Usually, substances that dissolve the easiest will move up the paper the most. If an ink dissolves completely, it will be carried with solvent all the way to the top of the paper. Try this with a washable marker and water.

How well the ink sticks to the paper. Inks that are strongly attached to the filter paper will not move up the paper much.

The length of the paper. The separation of the different dyes along the paper increases if the solvent is allowed to carry the ink up a longer distance. At the beginning of the experiment, the colors are all bundled together. As the solvent moves up the paper, the separation of the spots becomes greater and greater. Note, however, that the order of the colors does not change with the distance traveled.

Each spot in a chromatograph represents a different component of the original ink solution. The pattern that is created is like a fingerprint for identifying the original ink. That's why chromatography is used by forensic scientists to identify criminals by breaking down the ink used in notes and letters to trace the pattern to the criminal's pen.

> ### Explore Further
> Try using chromatography to analyze other evidence that may be found at a crime scene, such as lipstick. Try markers or other types and colors of pens.

Handwriting Analysis

Some criminals forge documents, hoping that people will think the documents are genuine and that someone else wrote them. Your handwriting is as unique as your fingerprints—from how you dot your i's to the way you connect the letters. It's hard to disguise your handwriting because you don't think about how you're writing something—you're too busy thinking about what you're writing.

Problem

How can a forged signature be identified using handwriting analysis?

Experiment Summary

You'll attempt to forge a signature and use handwriting analysis to compare it to the genuine signature.

What You Need

- ○ Paper
- ○ Pen
- ○ Parent or some other volunteer to provide the genuine signature
- ○ Ruler
- ○ Tracing paper or tissue paper

Top of Letter Analysis

Bottom of Letter Analysis

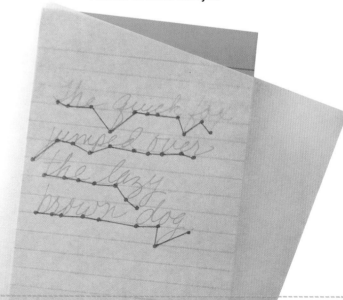

Experimental Procedure

1. Ask your volunteer to sign their name three times on a piece of paper, one under the other. Notice that the signatures are not identical. Most people have small variations in their signature, but the general features are the same.

2. On a separate piece of paper, practice copying the signature until you feel you can make a passable copy. Select your three best forgeries to analyze.

3. Examine the genuine and forged signatures using top of letter, bottom of letter, slant, and spacing analysis.

Conclusion

How closely did your forged signature resemble the genuine signature in each of the four analyses? Could these tests be used to expose a forged signature? Could you improve your forged signature based on these results?

Top of Letter Analysis

1. Place the tracing paper or tissue paper over the genuine signature.

2. Make a dot on the tracing paper at the highest points on each of the letters in the signature.

3. Use the ruler to connect the dots, creating a zigzag line across the top of the signature.

4. Compare this line to the line created by analyzing the forged signatures to see if they are similar.

Bottom of Letter Analysis

1. Place the tracing paper or tissue paper over the genuine signature.

2. Make a dot on the tracing paper at the lowest points on each of the letters in the signature.

3. Use the ruler to connect the dots, creating a zigzag line across the bottom of the signature.

4. Compare this line to the line created by analyzing the forged signatures to see if they are similar.

Spacing Analysis

1. Place the tracing paper or tissue paper over the genuine signature.

2. Make a dot on the tracing paper at the low points at the beginning and end of each letter in the signature.

3. Use the ruler to connect the ending dot for each letter to the starting dot of the next letter, creating a series of short lines that represent the size of the space between each letter.

4. Compare the lines to the lines created by analyzing the forged signatures to see if they are similar.

Slant Analysis

1. Place the tracing paper or tissue paper over the genuine signature.

2. Use the ruler to make a line with the same angle as the letter through each letter in the signature.

3. Compare the series of lines to the lines created by analyzing the forged signatures to see if they are similar.

Spacing Analysis

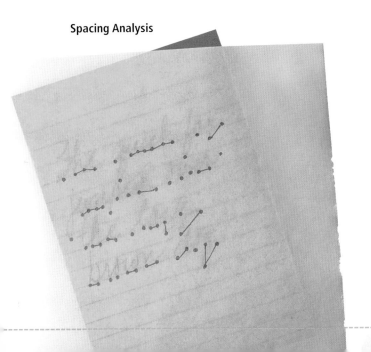

Slant Analysis

Take a Closer Look

When the police suspect forgery, they often collect handwriting samples, called *exemplars,* from suspects and compare them to the questioned document using the same techniques used in this experiment. Even though no one writes exactly the same way twice, your handwriting contains many identifiable features including where the pen first touches the paper or leaves the paper when a particular letter is written or whether you write darker or lighter when the pen moves downwards. These features are even more apparent when observed under a microscope.

There are many factors that influence how you write. These include:

- The writing utensil and surface
- Your age and how long you have been writing
- How fast you write
- What type of writing you learned in school
- What other languages you know
- Your nationality

Rather than trying to copy someone's handwriting, criminals may just try to disguise their own writing. In that case, forensic handwriting analysts must decide if someone is trying to change his handwriting as well as who that someone is. Analysts will also look at word choice and writing style for additional clues. The most popular way to disguise handwriting is to switch hands, but the handwriting is still similar enough to that of the other hand to be identified.

The victims of autograph forgers, such as celebrities and sports stars, now have a weapon to protect themselves. The *DNA pen* mixes the owner's saliva with the ink so that any autograph written with the pen contains a bit of their DNA. This could be the ultimate tool for authenticating an autograph!

Don't confuse forensic handwriting analysis with *graphology.* Graphology is a pseudoscience in which a person's character and personality are supposedly revealed in their handwriting. For example, graphologists claim that secretive people lean their writing a little backwards to indicate withdrawal from others and make their signature illegible so you won't know who wrote it. Forensic handwriting analysis involves handwriting comparison to determine authorship and examination of the document as a whole, including the paper and ink. Graphology isn't considered admissible in court, but the scientific findings of a forensic handwriting analyst are considered key evidence in cases involving written documents.

Sherlock Holmes

Below is an excerpt of "Norwood Builder" by Sir Arthur Conan Doyle, in which Sherlock Holmes uses handwriting analysis to help unravel a mysterious death.

Holmes had picked up the pages, which formed the rough draft of the will in question, and was looking at them with the keenest interest upon his face.

"There are some points about that document, Lestrade, are there not?" said he, pushing them over.

The official looked at them with a puzzled expression.

"I can read the first few lines and these in the middle of the second page, and one or two at the end. Those are as clear as print," said he, "but the writing in between is very bad, and there are three places where I cannot read it at all."

"What do you make of that?" said Holmes.

"Well, what do you make of it?"

Can you account for the unusual writing in the document? Take a moment to try to figure it out before reading Sherlock Holmes' analysis.

"That it was written in a train. The good writing represents stations, the bad writing movement, and the very bad writing passing over points. A scientific expert would pronounce at once that this was drawn up on a suburban line, since nowhere save in the immediate vicinity of a great city could there be so quick a succession of points. Granting that his whole journey was occupied in drawing up the will, then the train was an express, only stopping once between Norwood and London Bridge."

Document Recovery

A bank robber throws the note he wrote instructing the bank teller to empty the vault into a fire. An embezzler burns the receipts that prove he stole thousands of dollars. These criminals think they've destroyed the incriminating evidence, but they're wrong. The contents of these documents can often be recovered if the paper hasn't burned away completely. Handling burned and charred documents can be a very difficult and delicate job for forensic scientists.

Problem

How does the writing device determine how well information can be recovered from a burnt document?

Experiment Summary

You'll burn paper with writing in different types of ink on it and then try to recover the information.

What You Need

- ○ Measuring cups
- ○ Glycerin (can be found at drug stores)
- ○ Water
- ○ Spray bottle
- ○ White paper
- ○ Volunteer
- ○ Black pen
- ○ 2 aluminum pie plates
- ○ Matches
- ○ Bucket of sand
- ○ Cookie sheet
- ○ Tongs
- ○ Black pencil
- ○ Black marker
- ○ Black crayon
- ○ Infrared light or heat lamp (optional)

Experimental Procedure

1. Mix ½ cup (125 ml) of glycerin and 1½ cups (375 ml) of water in the spray bottle. Shake it up well so that the water and glycerin mix.

2. On a piece of paper, have a friend use the pen to write a secret message in large letters. The message should cover most of the paper. When she's finished, she should scrunch the paper into a tight ball.

3. Put the balled-up paper in the middle of one of the aluminum plates. Take both plates and the cookie sheet outside. Place the one with the paper in it on the driveway or a clear patch of sidewalk. Put the bucket of sand nearby. (If the fire gets out of hand, you can use the sand to put it out.)

4. Use a match to light the paper on fire. It will make a lot of smoke. Wait for the fire to burn out. If the paper continues to smolder, cover it with the second pie plate to help it stop burning.

5. Let the paper cool down. When the paper is cool, gently transfer it to the cookie sheet with the tongs.

6. Carefully spray the burned paper with the glycerin-water mixture in the spray bottle until the paper is completely wet. Gently spread and smooth out the paper on the cookie sheet. Spray the paper again if needed.

7. Carefully observe the paper. Can you read any of the writing on the paper? Tilt the cookie sheet so the light hits the paper at different angles. Record your observations.

8. Repeat steps 2 through 7 with the pencil, marker, and crayon. Be sure to use the same secret message.

9. If you have an infrared light or heat lamp, shine it on the ash and burned paper. Can you read the writing any better? (Burnt ink and pencil reflect this light more than the burnt paper does.)

Conclusion

From which paper were you able to recover the most writing? From which did you recover the least amount of writing? Were you able to figure out the secret message? Did you run into any problems working with the burned documents?

Take a Closer Look

The glycerin and water solution is used to soften the burned document so that it can be flattened without falling to pieces. Forensic scientists use a solution similar to the one in this experiment. They may also add other chemicals, such as alcohol and chloral hydrate, to help soften the paper.

Once the document has been flattened, any remaining ink on the paper can be read. Most ink contains dyes with small amounts of metal. The metal usually survives the fire. Anything written with these inks can still be read once the paper is flattened.

If the writing still isn't completely visible, it can be photographed with infrared film. This film records infrared light. Infrared light has a wavelength just longer than what we are able to see. The metal and dyes reflect the infrared light more than the visible light we see, making the writing more clear. These photographs of the burned documents can then be used as evidence.

As you may have noticed in this experiment, burned and charred documents are very fragile. They must be handled with extreme care and are often hand-delivered to the laboratory in a cotton or wool-lined box so that no further damage is done.

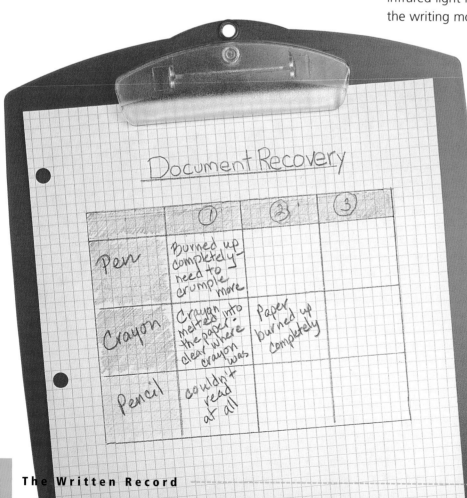

Document Recovery

	①	②	③
Pen	Burned up completely—need to crumple more		
Crayon	Crayon melted into the paper: clear where crayon was	Paper burned up completely	
Pencil	couldn't read at all		

FORENSIC CAREERS

Questioned Document Examiner (QDE)

If you like chemistry and are good at noticing details, then you might want to be a questioned document examiner. A paper associated with a crime is called a "questioned document." The document can be hand-written, typed, printed, or copied on just about anything that can take words, including paper, walls, or even clothes. Examples of questioned documents are wills, contracts, paper money, ransom notes, stamps, driver's licenses, paintings, and date books. These documents become "questioned documents" when investigators aren't sure if they're genuine or have been altered, coun-terfeited, or forged. Sometimes they just want to figure out who wrote them. Questioned documents can also reveal other clues that have nothing to do with forgeries. The paper and ink used, fingerprints, and other evidence not visible to the eye can help lead investigators to the bad guys.

What Do QDEs Do?

- Find out whether a document is authentic.
- Find out if the person who was supposed to have made the document really made it when they were supposed to have made it.
- Find out if a document has been changed in any way.
- Compare handwriting, signatures, and typed documents.
- Find out the ages and sources of the paper and inks.

- Recover writing from damaged documents that have been burned, soaked, or crumpled.

How Do They Do It?

- Check documents for fingerprints (see page 49).
- Look for identifying marks from the typewriter, printer, copy machine, fax machine, or whatever may have made the document. These machines usually have very small defects that leave marks on the paper. These marks can help QDEs identify exactly what machine made the document.
- Analyze the ink using chromatography (see page 68) and other chemical tests to identify its source.
- Analyze the ink on the paper to determine if the docu-ment has been changed. Infrared and ultraviolet lights often reveal differences in inks or if marks have been erased that indicate the document has been altered.
- Look for indentations that have been left when some-one writes on a piece of paper over the document in question. QDEs never rub a pencil over the paper to expose the writing, as this would damage the evi-dence. Instead, they look at the document when lit from the side or back—try it out!
- Compare the handwriting on handwritten questioned documents to known samples to determine who wrote the document.

How Can I Become a QDE?

To become a QDE, you need to have excellent vision and you can't be color blind. There is no college degree in questioned document examination, but it's a good idea to get a degree in criminalistics, forensic science, chem-istry, biology, or some other related field. Then you want to find a job in a forensics laboratory working with a cer-tified QDE as an apprentice. After two years, you'll be eli-gible to be certified by The American Board of Forensic Document Examiners.

Left Behind

Every criminal, no matter how careful she's being, leaves something behind at the crime scene. This could be the tire tracks from her car, bits of dirt she tracked in, or fibers from her clothes. Forensic scientists carefully gather and analyze this evidence to track the criminal down.

Identifying Chemicals

In order to solve crimes, forensic chemists often need to identify poisons, gunshot residue, and other chemicals. Color, odor, texture, pH, and reaction to other substances are unique for individual chemicals and can help to identify important clues. A forensic chemist will observe each of these properties to gather information about a chemical's identity.

Problem

How can common substances be identified by their chemical properties?

Experiment Summary

You'll observe the properties of common substances, including their color, odor, texture, pH, and reactions with water, vinegar, and iodine.

Sugar Molecule

What You Need

- Baking soda
- Black paper
- Magnifying glass
- Measuring spoons
- 24 small cups
- Dropper
- Vinegar
- Iodine solution (found at most drug stores)
- Water
- pH indicator (see the recipe on page 78)
- Cornstarch
- Plaster of Paris
- Sugar
- Table salt

pH Indicator Recipe

What You Need

- 6 red cabbage leaves
- 2-quart saucepan
- Water
- Stove
- Colander or strainer
- Jar with a lid

What You Do

1. Tear the red cabbage leaves into small pieces and put them in a saucepan with 2 cups of water.

2. With the help of an adult, heat the water and cabbage and leave on the stove. Let them boil for 10 minutes. Wait for the liquid to cool.

3. Use the colander to strain the leaves from the liquid and pour the liquid into a jar. Seal the jar and store it in the refrigerator. The pH indicator will be good for one week. If you want to keep it longer (up to six weeks), place it in the freezer and thaw it before you use it.

Experimental Procedure

1. Place a pinch of baking soda on a piece of black paper. Use the magnifying glass to study the particles. Are the particles large or small? What shape are they? Record your observations.

2. Pinch some of the baking soda between your fingers and rub your fingers together to observe how it feels. Is the texture smooth or gritty? Does the powder stick to your fingers? Record your observations.

3. Does the baking soda have a smell? If so, be sure to record it.

4. Place 1 teaspoon of the baking soda in a cup. With the dropper, put four drops of water on the baking soda and observe what happens. Does it soak in or stay as a drop on top of the powder? Is there any reaction? Do you see bubbles or a color change? Hold the cup in your hand to feel if there is a temperature change. Record your observations.

5. Put another teaspoon of baking soda in a clean cup. This time, add four drops of vinegar. Record your observations as you did in step 4.

6. In a third cup, put another teaspoon of baking soda and add four drops of iodine solution. Again, record your observations as you did in step 4.

7. In another cup, mix 1 teaspoon of baking soda with 1 tablespoon of water. Add four drops of pH indicator. Record the color of the solution.

8. Repeat steps 1 through 7 to test the cornstarch, plaster of Paris, sugar, and salt.

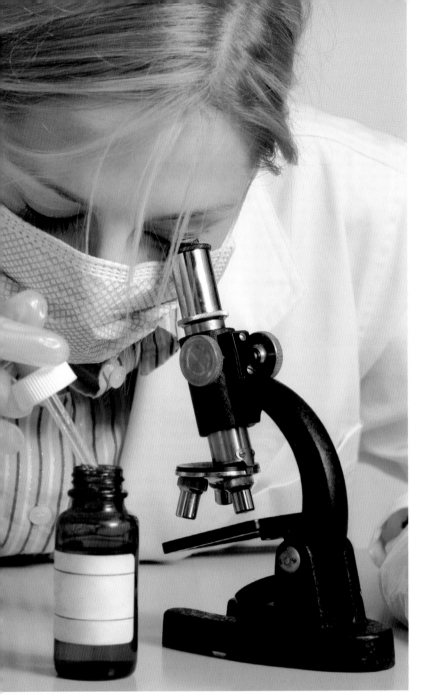

Forensic chemists often have the task of identifying chemicals or other substances found at crime scenes. Often these unknown substances are illegal drugs, and the findings of the crime lab can determine the guilt or innocence of a suspect. The scientists use a variety of tests, like the ones in this experiment, to figure out what a chemical is.

For example, if you want to determine if a powder is gunshot residue, first you have to find a positive test that proves a powder is gunshot residue, and then you can run that test on your unknown powder. It's also important to run more than one test on an unknown chemical so you're certain of its identity beyond a reasonable doubt.

In this experiment, four tests are run on the substances using water, vinegar, iodine, and pH indicator. Water was added to the substances to see if they would dissolve. All of the substances used dissolve in water but some, like cornstarch and plaster of Paris, make a milky paste. Vinegar was used to determine if the substances react with acids (vinegar is also known as acetic acid). Iodine is used to determine if starches are present; it turns a dark purple in the presence of starch. The pH indicator reveals if the substance is an acid or a base. The indicator turns red or pink in an acid and green or blue in a base.

Explore Further

Observe the properties of other white powders such as talcum powder, cream of tartar, or baking powder. Read the safety warnings on the packages before smelling or touching any chemicals.

Conclusion

Make a table of your results for each of the substances. Do any two of the substances have the exact same properties? That is, did they look, feel, smell, or react the same way? Would you be able to identify these substances or chemicals at a crime scene with these methods? Were any of your results surprising?

Fractography

Forensic scientists usually find all sorts of broken objects at a crime scene. Fractography is the study of how things break. Scientists can use the pieces to figure out how objects were broken. In order to understand how things break, you need to break things yourself and observe what happens.

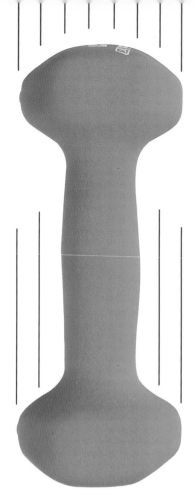

Problem

How does the force of an impact affect the breaking pattern of a ceramic tile?

Experiment Summary

You'll drop a weight on ceramic tiles from different heights and analyze the resulting break pattern.

What You Need

○ **Newspaper**

○ **12 ceramic tiles, 12 inches square (30 x 30 cm)**

○ **Meter stick or yardstick**

○ **Pencil**

○ **Helper**

○ **5-pound (2-kilo) dumbbell**

○ **Paper and pencil or camera**

Experimental Procedure

1. Spread the newspaper out on the sidewalk to catch all of the broken tile pieces. Be sure to wear closed-toe shoes while performing this experiment. The broken tiles may be sharp!

2. Use the meter stick to find the center of each tile and mark it with the pencil.

3. Place one of the tiles in the middle of the newspaper and have your helper carefully hold the meter stick near the center of the tile, perpendicular to the tile and to the floor.

4. Carefully hold the dumbbell next to the meter stick, also perpendicular to the floor, so that the bottom is 25 cm (10 inches) from the tile.

5. Release the dumbbell so that it falls and hits the center of the tile. The tile should break, or at least crack.

6. Use the paper and pencil to sketch or take a photo of the crack pattern on the tile. Be as detailed as possible.

Record the height you dropped the dumbbell from and, if the tile broke, how many pieces it broke into.

7. Repeat steps 4 through 6 three more times so that you drop the dumbbell on four tiles from a height of 25 cm (10 inches).

8. Repeat steps 4 through 7, first dropping the dumbbell from 50 cm (19.5 inches) and then dropping it from 100 cm (39.5 inches).

Conclusion

Describe the pattern of breaks for each distance you dropped the dumbbell. Were the breaks jagged or smooth? Straight or branching? What other characteristics did you observe?

Did the number of pieces the tile broke into vary with the height from which you dropped the dumbbell? Which height gave the greatest number of pieces? Which height gave the fewest?

The force with which the dumbbell hits the tile is in direct square root relationship to how high you drop it from. This means that to double the force, you need to drop the dumbbell from four times as high. For example,

dropping the dumbbell from 100 cm gives double the force of dropping it from 25 cm. To get three times the force, you would have to drop the dumbbell from 225 cm. What effect did doubling and quadrupling the distance have on the pattern of breaks and number of pieces in the broken tiles? What do you think would happen if you dropped the dumbbell from 225 cm, which is nine times the distance of your first drop? Try it out!

Take a Closer Look

Ceramics (like the tile), glass, and some plastics are all called brittle materials because they form cracks, or fractures, and break rather than stretch when a force is applied. Material engineers (scientists who work with materials and try to make them better) consider three types of forces: *tension,* or pulling forces; *compression,* or pushing forces; and *shearing,* when two surfaces are pulled in opposite directions. This experiment studies compression forces.

Brittle materials like the tiles break when a crack starts at a specific point and grows. Some cracks grow slowly from a small continuous force, such as a crack in a windshield on a car. Other cracks grow very quickly and it might look like the object explodes, such as when you drop a glass jar on the kitchen floor. In both cases, what the object is made of determines how the crack progresses and what break pattern appears.

Explore Further

Compare the breaking pattern of different sizes and thicknesses of ceramic tiles. Try breaking other brittle materials, such as glass and plastic. How do the cracking pattern and number of pieces vary for these materials? How are they similar and how are they different? What happens if you break the tile with something besides a dropped dumbbell? Try using a hammer and nail to break the tile. Break the tile off-center and see how that affects the breaking pattern.

Soil Analysis

Soil and dirt found at a crime scene and on suspects can provide clues to link them because soil is easily (and often unknowingly) carried from the crime scene. Forensic geologists will collect soil from shoes, clothing, car tires, tools, and, of course, the ground, and then use many different methods to determine if two soil samples come from the same place.

Problem

How does soil composition depend on location?

Experiment Summary

You'll collect soil samples from different locations and analyze their composition by soil layering.

What You Need

- Spade
- Map
- Pencil
- Ruler
- 4 reclosable plastic bags

- Permanent marker
- Magnifying glass
- White paper
- Black paper
- 4 soda bottles, 2 liters each

- Scissors (optional)
- Funnel
- Paint stirring stick (optional)
- Water
- Camera (optional)

Experimental Procedure

1. Collect soil samples from four different locations. Find locations that are as different from each other as possible. Mark these locations on your map.

2. Use your spade to dig up about 2 to 3 cups (0.5 to 0.7 liters) of soil from each location. You should dig about 4 to 6 inches (10 to 15 cm) deep and include any leaves or other debris that may be on the ground where you are digging. Put the samples in a plastic bag and label them with the marker.

3. Record your observations about each location. Include the amount of vegetation, how close it is to man-made structures like buildings or pavement, if it's heavily traveled, and anything else that you think might influence what's in the soil.

4. Use the magnifying glass to carefully examine each soil sample. Put some of the soil out on white and black paper so there is better contrast for the light and dark parts of the soil. Record your observations. Which parts of the soils are similar and which are different? Pay careful attention to color and texture.

5. Label the soda bottles with the locations and transfer the soil into the bottles with the funnel. If some pieces don't fit through the top of the bottle, cut it off with the scissors.

6. Fill the bottles with water so that there is at least 3 inches of water above the soil. Shake the bottle vigorously (or stir it with the paint stirring stick, if you had to cut off the top) so that the soil is broken up and floating in the water. Let the bottles sit undisturbed for at least 24 hours or until the dirt stops *precipitating* (falling out of the water) and has formed layers.

7. Sketch a picture or take a close-up photo of the layers of soil formed in each of the bottles.

Conclusion

How were the layers of soil in the bottles similar and how were they different? Does this agree with your observations with the magnifying glass? Did any of the bottles form layers not found in the other bottles? Were any of the layers found in all four bottles? If soil were found in a suspect's car, would you be able to tell if it came from one of the four sites where you collected soil?

How many different layers can you see?

Take a Closer Look

Soil is more than just dirt. It can contain all sorts of things, such as rocks, minerals, vegetation, animal matter, glass, manufactured objects, asphalt, brick fragments, and paint chips. Forensic geologists collect soil samples from the ground with a spade as in the experiment above. But, for surface dirt and dust, simple tape is used to collect a sample and, for cars, clothing, and other objects where the soil may be more deeply imbedded, a vacuum is used. In any case, of all the evidence at a crime scene, soil needs to be collected first, as it is easily contaminated.

Most forensic geologists usually examine soil samples with a magnifying glass and microscope first to compare color and texture. In fact, color is the main factor in identifying soil location. The presence of certain minerals in the soil can give it a distinctive color. For example, the presence of copper minerals gives a green color, while black soil points to the presence of manganese and iron. If further observations are needed, forensic geologists will use a layering technique similar to the one in this experiment. Other methods are used to measure pH and mineral content. Biological matter found in soil, such as hairs, pollen, or seeds, is also investigated.

Sherlock Holmes

Even Sherlock Holmes used observations of soil color to help solve crimes, as shown in this excerpt from The Sign of Four by Arthur Conan Doyle.

"It is simplicity itself," he remarked, chuckling at my surprise—"so absurdly simple that an explanation is superfluous; and yet it may serve to define the limits of observation and of deduction. Observation tells me that you have a little reddish mould adhering to your instep. Just opposite the Wigmore Street Office they have taken up the pavement and thrown up some earth, which lies in such a way that it is difficult to avoid treading in it in entering. The earth is of this peculiar reddish tint which is found, as far as I know, nowhere else in the neighbourhood. So much is observation."

Explore Further

Collect soil from other sites to add to your collection. Contact the Geological Survey for your state and get a soil map for your area. Do the soil types in your sample match the soil types on the soil map?

Test the pH of each of your soil samples. pH is a measure of how acidic or basic a material is. The pH scale runs from one to 14, with one being the most acidic, seven being neutral, and 14 being the most basic. To measure the pH of soil, mix the soil with an equal amount of water, for example 1 cup of soil mixed with 1 cup of water. Shake the soil and water together well and dip a pH strip, found at most aquarium or pet stores, in the soil-water mixture. A color change on the strip will indicate the pH of the soil.

Tire Tracks

After committing a crime, most criminals try to get away so they don't get caught, either on foot or in a vehicle such as a car or bicycle. Luckily, each of these can leave some sort of print that can help identify the bad guy, or at least the vehicle he used to get away. Forensic scientists who specialize in identifying and matching tire prints need to recognize how different conditions, such as temperature, surfaces, or tire pressure, change a tire's print.

Problem

How does the air pressure in a bicycle tire affect the print produced?

Experiment Summary

You'll compare the width and patterns of bicycle tire prints made at three different tire pressures.

What You Need

- White paper
- Carbon paper*
- Tape
- Bicycle

- Tire pump with gauge
- Helper who weighs more than 130 pounds (59 kg)
- Ruler

*Available at office supply stores

Experimental Procedure

1. Place a piece of carbon paper between two pieces of white paper and tape them together.

2. Inflate the back tire of the bicycle as much as you can and record the reading on the gauge.

3. On a flat smooth surface, such as your driveway or the street, have your helper prepare to ride the bicycle. Place the carbon paper sandwich just behind the front wheel of the bicycle so that the carbon side is facing up between the two pieces of paper.

4. Have your helper ride forward so the back wheel of the bicycle rides over the paper. (The more your helper weighs, the clearer the print will be.)

5. Untape the papers and, on the paper with the tire print, write down the reading of the tire pump gauge you recorded in step 2. If you can't get a good print, try using a helper who weighs more or finding a smoother surface to ride the bicycle on.

6. Repeat steps 3 through 5 until you have at least three good prints of the fully inflated tire.

7. Deflate the rear tire of the bicycle so that it feels about halfway inflated. Do not use the gauge to determine the halfway point, as a fully deflated tire does not have 0 air pressure. (If your tire is empty, the gauge will show 15 PSI—this is the force of the air pressure all around you.) Record the reading on the gauge, though, so you know what the air pressure is.

8. Repeat steps 3 through 6 for the halfway deflated tire, then deflate the tire all the way, record the air pressure, and do it all over again.

9. Measure the width of all the tire prints and calculate the average width at each tire pressure.

10. Record any observations you have about the tread pattern on the print and if there are any changes in this pattern as the tire pressure is changed.

Conclusion

Make a line graph of tire width versus tire pressure. How did the width of the tire vary with pressure? Would you be able to tell if a bicycle tire was inflated from its tire print? What other observations were you able to make about the tire print as the air pressure was decreased?

In general, tires leave behind three types of prints. The easiest to recognize are *visible prints.* These occur when the tires run through something like oil, paint, or mud and leave a track. *Latent* tire prints are not visible to the eye but can be seen using a variety of techniques (see Try This!). For example, tire manufacturers use extender oils to make the tire rubber more flexible. These oils may be left on concrete or paved roads and can be seen and photographed with ultraviolet lights. The most useful prints are *plastic,* or three-dimensional impressions made in sand, soil, snow, or some other soft surface.

Once forensic scientists have collected a tire print from a crime scene, they try to figure out which vehicle made the print. There are several features that help identify tires, such as the pattern of the tire tread. Most tires have two or three rows of tread that run along the tire called ribs. The channels that run between the ribs are called grooves. Between the parts of the ribs, there may be shallower channels called sipes. Along the outside edge of the tire, there are raised sections called lugs with channels between them called slots. These parts of the tread have two purposes: to increase traction in water by guiding water into the grooves and away from the tire through the slots, and to reduce the noise made by tires as you drive on the road.

Groove

Slot

Lug

Try This!

Latent Tire Prints

Sometimes a car used in a crime leaves prints that are difficult to photograph or even see. These latent prints may occur when a car drives over a piece of cardboard or some other smooth surface and leaves a dusting of dirt. The print can be lifted off this smooth surface using carbon paper and static electricity.

What You Need

- Bicycle
- Helper who weight more than 130 pounds (59 kg)
- Cardboard or poster board
- Carbon paper
- Tape
- Fur or a wool sweater

What You Do

1. Ride the bicycle around so that the tires are dirty but not muddy. Then have your helper ride over the piece of cardboard or poster board so that you leave a latent print.

2. Carefully lay a piece of carbon paper, carbon side down, where the bicycle ran over the cardboard. Secure the corners with tape.

3. Lightly brush the fur or wool sweater across the top of the carbon paper for 30 seconds. Be careful not to press the carbon paper against the cardboard. The fur will pull electrons off the paper, causing the paper to become positively charged. The charged paper will attract the dirt and dust particles left by the latent tire print.

4. Gently remove the carbon paper from the cardboard to see the tire print transferred onto the carbon.

Sherlock Holmes

The following is an excerpt from "The Adventure of the Priory School" by Sir Arthur Conan Doyle in which the hero, Sherlock Holmes, analyzes a bicycle tire track to help track down a thief.

We had come on a small black ribbon of pathway. In the middle of it, clearly marked on the sodden soil, was the track of a bicycle.

"Hurrah!" I cried. "We have it."

But Holmes was shaking his head, and his face was puzzled and expectant rather than joyous.

"A bicycle, certainly, but not the bicycle," said he. "I am familiar with forty-two different impressions left by tyres. This, as you perceive, is a Dunlop, with a patch upon the outer cover. Heidegger's tyres were Palmers, leaving longitudinal stripes. Aveling, the mathematical master, was sure upon the point. Therefore, it is not Heidegger's track."

"The boy's, then?"

"Possibly, if we could prove a bicycle to have been in his possession. But this we have utterly failed to do. This track, as you perceive, was made by a rider who was going from the direction of the school."

"Or towards it?"

"No, no, my dear Watson. The more deeply sunk impression is, of course, the hind wheel, upon which the weight rests. You perceive several places where it has passed across and obliterated the more shallow mark of the front one. It was undoubtedly heading away from the school. It may or may not be connected with our inquiry, but we will follow it backwards before we go any farther."

Explore Further

Compare the tracks made by different bicycles. Does the surface the bicycle is riding on affect the tire print? What about the weight of the rider? What other factors do you think would affect the print produced by a bicycle tire?

Glass

While a pile of broken glass may not resemble the object it originally formed, to a forensic scientist there are plenty of clues to help reconstruct the item and what caused it to break. The shape, size, number of pieces, and how they are distributed can give hints as to how the object was broken (see page 80), the density of the glass, and other characteristics. This information helps forensic scientists narrow down what the object was or what it was used for. For example, headlight glass found at a crime scene can help forensic scientists identify the make and model of a get-away car.

Problem

How is the type of glass and what it's used for related to its density?

Experiment Summary

You'll measure the density of several types of glass.

What You Need

- ◯ **Wide mouth jar**
- ◯ **Glass samples:** large glass marble, dropper (remove the rubber bulb), eyeglasses lens, baby food jar, Pyrex test tube
- ◯ **Water**
- ◯ **Permanent marker**
- ◯ **Graduated cylinder**
- ◯ **Food scale**
- ◯ **Calculator**

Experimental Procedure

1. Place the tallest glass sample in the jar and pour water in the jar so that the top of the water is at least 1 inch (3 cm) over the glass sample. Tap the side of the jar to make sure there are no bubbles in the water.

2. Carefully mark the water line on the jar with the permanent marker.

3. Pour out the water and remove the glass sample. Dry the jar completely. Fill the empty jar with water so that it is exactly to the line. Again, make sure there are no bubbles in the water.

4. Measure the volume of the water in milliliters by carefully pouring it into the graduated cylinder. It is important to be as precise as possible. Record the volume of water that fills the jar to the line you made in step 2.

5. Dry the glass jar and place the first glass sample inside. Again, fill the jar to the water line, making sure there are no bubbles or air in the water or the glass sample.

6. Measure and record the volume of the water in the jar with glass sample in milliliters by pouring the water into the graduated cylinder.

7. Calculate and record the volume of the glass sample by subtracting the volume of water in the jar with the sample (from step 6) from the volume of water in the empty jar (from step 4).

8. Repeat steps 5 through 7 at least five times for each of the samples, and calculate the average volume of each sample.

9. Use the food scale to measure the mass of each of the samples in grams at least five times, and calculate the average.

10. Calculate the density in grams/milliliter of each sample by dividing its average mass by its average volume.

Conclusion

Make a bar graph showing the density of each of your samples. Do any of your samples have the same or similar densities? What is the range of the densities? (That is: What is the highest and lowest density?) Do you see any connection between the density of the glass and its purpose?

Did any of the samples give more precise values for density than others? If the samples gave a wide range of values for volume and mass during any of the five trials, then its value for density is less precise than a sample that had very similar values for volume and density over the five trials. You may notice that smaller items give less precise values than larger items.

Take a Closer Look

The density of an object doesn't change when it's broken into pieces, which makes it ideal for identifying glass.

Density is a ratio of an object's mass to its volume and can be calculated using the equation Density = Mass/Volume. You can think of density as how much mass or "stuff" is crammed into a space or volume. If you compare a glass ball to a styrofoam ball, you can tell that the styrofoam is less dense because it has much less mass for the same volume or size.

Glass is made by melting and cooling a mixture of lime, soda, silicon oxides (or sand), and different metal oxides. For example, window glass contains sodium, calcium, magnesium, and aluminum oxides, while automobile headlights and Pyrex glass contain boron oxides to make them heat resistant. These various metal oxides used in different types of glass account for the unique densities.

Most glass found at crime scenes is in the form of tiny slivers or fragments, which makes it difficult to analyze using the method in this experiment. To test the density of very small glass samples, forensic scientists place the glass in different liquids with known densities. The glass will float if it's less dense than the liquid and it will sink if it's more dense than the liquid. Scientists test the glass in pairs of liquids until they find a combination where the glass sample doesn't float or sink but sits right in the middle of the two liquids. The density of the glass can then be calculated using the densities of the two liquids.

Explore Further

Try investigating the density of one type of glass from different sources such as mirrors or windows. (Be very careful when dealing with broken glass. Wear gloves or use tweezers to handle broken glass so you don't cut yourself.) Visit a junkyard and see if you can find glass from the headlights of different cars. Can you identify the car from the density of its glass?

Index of Refraction

Another property that can be used to identify glass is index of refraction. The *index of refraction* is a measure of how much light bends in the glass and can be calculated by dividing the speed of light in a vacuum by the speed of light in the glass or other material. In general, denser glasses have a higher index of refraction and bend light more than less dense glass. Diamonds have a very high index of refraction, and their ability to bend light gives them the sparkle that makes them so valuable.

If you place a piece of glass or other clear object in a liquid with the same index of refraction, it's almost impossible to see the object! This is because they both bend light the same amount, so you can't tell where the liquid ends and the object begins.

Pour water into a clear drinking glass and put a Pyrex test tube in the water. Even though the glass, water, and test tube are all clear, you can see each because the drinking glass, water, and test tube all have different indices of refraction, so they bend the light differently, especially at their edges.

Empty the glass and dry it thoroughly. Put the test tube inside (it has to be Pyrex to work) and pour vegetable oil in the glass and in the test tube. It looks like the test tube has disappeared! Vegetable oil and Pyrex have almost the exact same index of refraction, so the light doesn't bend at all when traveling from the oil to the Pyrex and back out again.

Insects in the Soil

Criminals often overlook the most unlikely clues. The bugs that might attach themselves to clothes and other items can provide powerful evidence. Forensic entomologists, scientists who study insects as they relate to crime, need to be able to recognize when an insect is out of place to take advantage of these tiny clues.

Problem

How does the environment affect what kinds of insects live there?

Experiment Summary

You'll collect insects from three different sites in your neighborhood using a Berlese funnel and compare the variety of species you find.

What You Need

- Bucket
- Spade
- Berlese Funnel (see page 95)
- Rubbing alcohol
- Magnifying glass
- Insect identification book
- Forceps or tweezers
- Magnifying glass
- White paper
- Black paper
- Microscope (optional)
- Gooseneck lamp with 40-watt light bulb (optional)

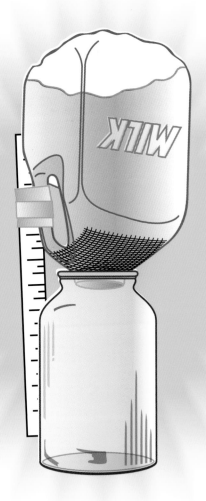

Make a Berlese Funnel

What You Need

- Empty plastic milk jug
- Scissors
- Large clear jar (at least 1 pint) with lid
- Ruler
- Masking tape
- $\frac{1}{4}$-inch-mesh window screen in a 6-inch (15 cm) square

What You Do

1. Cut the bottom out of the milk jug and turn it upside down over the jar to make a funnel.

2. Tape the ruler to the handle of the milk jug so it is just long enough to reach the outside bottom of the jar.

3. Cut four 1-inch slits in the window screen. These are to allow larger insects to crawl through.

4. Bend down the corners of the window screen and place it in the funnel (milk jug) so it fits snugly inside the bottom end.

Experimental Procedure

1. Select three sites to collect insects. These sites should be as diverse as possible. For example, you could select your front lawn, a wooded area, and the school playground.

2. Take your bucket to one of the sites and fill it with leaves, dirt, and whatever else is on the ground that might house insects. You'll probably find more insects if the ground cover is wet or damp, so try to do your collecting after it rains.

3. Put several handfuls of the leaves and dirt you just collected on top of the window screen in your Berlese funnel.

4. Pour rubbing alcohol in the bottom jar so it is about $\frac{1}{2}$ inch (1 cm) deep.

5. Carefully set the funnel on top of the jar and tape the ruler to the jar so it won't tip over.

6. Place the entire Berlese funnel in a warm place where it won't be disturbed. You may want to set the gooseneck lamp so that it shines into the funnel. The bulb should be at least 4 inches (10 cm) above the leaves.

7. Wait four or five days until the leaves dry out completely. As they dry, the insects and other critters will move down and fall into the alcohol, where they'll be preserved. When this has happened, carefully remove the milk jug and put the lid on the jar.

8. Separate the insects with the forceps or tweezers. Use the magnifying glass to study the insects you have collected and identify as many as you can with the insect identification book. Try placing the black paper underneath or behind the jar to see the lighter-colored insects and use white paper to better see the darker-colored insects. Record how many of each type of insect you found in your sample.

9. Repeat steps 2 through 8 for the other two sites.

Conclusion

How many insects were you able to identify in your samples? How many different types of insects did you find at each site? Did any of the sites have the same types of insects? Were there any insects that you found at only one of the sites?

You can find out how similar two sites are using *Jaccard's index*. To calculate Jaccard's index, first count how many different species of insects were found at only one of the sites, and call this number A. Then count how many of the same species of insects were found at both sites, and call this number B. You can then calculate Jaccard's index using the formula:

Jaccard's index = (A/B) x 100

For example, suppose you found 12 species at your first site and 14 species at the second site. If only three species were found at both sites, then 9+11=20 species were found at only one of the sites. In this case, Jaccard's Index would be (3/20) x 100 = 15 percent, which means that the two sites have 15 percent of their insects in common.

If two sites have all of the same species, then Jaccard's index would be 100 percent, and there would be no way to tell the two places apart by looking at the insects in the dirt and leaves. But, if two sites have none of the same insects, then Jaccard's index would be 0 percent.

Explore Further

Compare the insects found in the leaves and dirt for other contrasting sites, such as north and south-facing sides of a hill or different distances from a road or highway. Be sure to bring an adult with you when collecting samples from sites away from home.

Take a Closer Look

Insects make up the largest group of living things in the world. They're everywhere, and many of them are too small to see with the naked eye. Almost 1 million species of insects have been identified, but there are probably just as many that haven't been found yet. Some scientists say there are 200 million insects for every one person on the planet! Despite this, most insects are very specialized in where they choose to live. They may require specific types of soil or just the right amount of sunlight. This means that insects can help trace the path of important pieces of evidence, and even of the criminal themselves. In one case, police investigators brought the get-away car to an entomologist who used the insects caught in the grill to trace the path of the criminal across the country!

You.

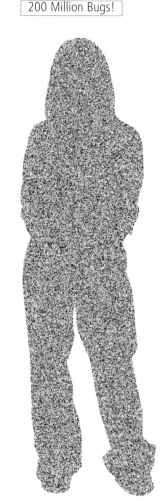

200 Million Bugs!

FORENSIC CAREERS

Forensic Entomologist

Any time a body or other evidence is found where insects abound, investigators are sure to collect as many bugs as they can find and send them to a forensic entomologist. This scientist specializes in bugs of all sorts, particularly identifying insects and their habitat. There are three fields of forensic entomology:

> **Urban entomology**—cases with insects that involve buildings and other man-made structures.

> **Stored products entomology**—cases where insects are found in foods and other products.

> **Medicolegal entomology**—when insects are used to determine the time, cause, or site of a death and the possible criminal misuse of insects.

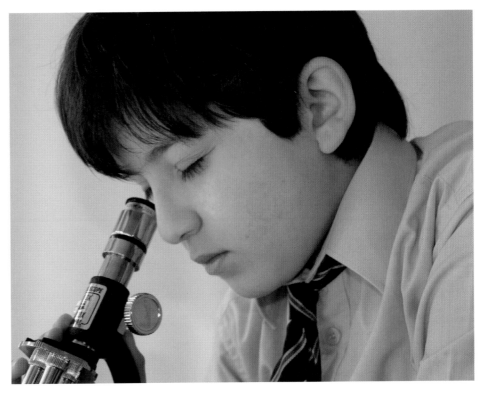

What Do Forensic Entomologists Do?

- Help determine the time of death in murder cases.
- Trace the path of illegal drugs smuggled into the country.
- Determine whether a body or other evidence has been moved from one place to another.

How Do They Do It?

- By studying the life cycles of maggots and other insect eggs under all sorts of conditions, forensic entomologists can narrow down the time of death to within a couple of hours.
- When criminals smuggle drugs, they also unknowingly smuggle insects. The types of insects can tell investigators where the drugs came from and where they've been. Illegal drugs like heroin or cocaine affect the development of maggots, and this can give investigators clues to when the drugs were moved.

How Can I Become a Forensic Entomologist?

If you like bugs and other creepy, crawly things, you might consider becoming a forensic entomologist. You'll need to go to college and get a degree in biology, zoology, or entomology and then keep going to school for a master's or doctoral degree in entomology. You'll also need to get certified by the American Board of Forensic Entomology. Jobs in forensic entomology are very hard to get, so most entomologists work at colleges or universities.

Insects in the Air

If you've ever been on a picnic, you know that flies are attracted to food. But they didn't show up for a snack—the flies lay their eggs in rotting meat and decaying vegetation.

Forensic entomologists use flies and their eggs, which become maggots when they hatch, to provide information about what occurred at crime scenes. The predictable sequence of the maggot life cycle can even tell them when certain events happened.

Problem

How does the kind of decaying food affect what type of insect is attracted to it?

Experiment Summary

You'll construct an insect trap and observe which insects are attracted to different baits.

What You Need

- ⚪ Insect Trap
- ⚪ ¼ lb (4 oz) raw beef liver
- ⚪ Thermometer
- ⚪ 1 quart (32 oz) disposable plastic storage container
- ⚪ Freezer
- ⚪ Forceps or tweezers
- ⚪ Insect identification book
- ⚪ ¼ lb (4 oz) cooked beef liver
- ⚪ Spinach leaves

Experimental Procedure

1. This experiment works best in warm weather (70°F [21.1°C] or warmer). Center the ¼ lb (4 oz) of raw beef liver in the bottom of the insect trap. Place the trap in an open area outdoors.

2. Use the thermometer to record the air temperature near the trap.

3. Leave the trap for at least six hours to collect insects.

4. Before removing the trap, measure and record the air temperature again near the trap. Carefully take off the bottom of the insect trap and replace it with a third storage container that has no holes. Throw away the beef liver.

5. Place the trap with the insects in a freezer for 24 hours to kill the insects without damaging them.

6. Remove the insects using forceps or tweezers and classify them with the insect identification book. Record how many of each species were collected.

7. Repeat steps 1 through 6 for the cooked beef liver and spinach leaves. Be sure to set the trap in the same place and at the same temperature, if possible.

Conclusion

Make a bar graph of the type and number of insects attracted by each of the baits. How did the total number of insects attracted by each of the baits compare? Which bait attracted the greatest variety of insects?

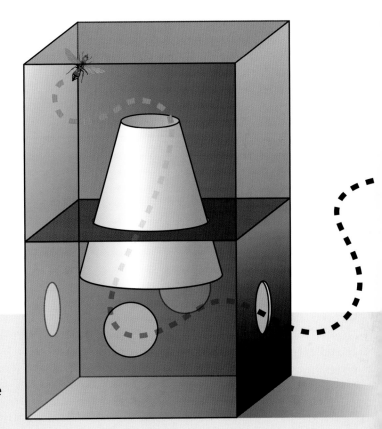

Make an Insect Trap

What You Need
- 2 disposable plastic storage containers with lids, 1 quart (30 oz) each
- Scissors
- Hot glue gun
- Overhead transparency
- Transparent tape
- Black paint

What You Do

1. Cut a 3-inch (8-cm) diameter hole in the center of the lids of the containers so they match up.

2. Use the hot glue gun to glue the lids together so that the insides are facing out and you can still attach the bottoms of the containers.

3. Cut the overhead transparency in quarters so you have a piece that measures about 4 by 5 inches (10 x 13 cm). Roll the transparency into a cone so that the small end has a 1-inch (2.5 cm) opening and the large end matches the hole in the container covers. Use the tape to secure the funnel to the hole in the covers. Trim the funnel as necessary so that it fits inside the container when it's attached to the lid with at least 1-inch (2.5 cm) clearance. With the scissors, cut 1-inch (2.5-cm) diameter holes in each side of one of the containers.

4. Paint the outside of the container with the holes black.

5. Attach the containers to the lids and funnel so that the funnel is in the clear container with no holes. The side that is painted black is the bottom of the trap. Insects will enter through the holes and fly upward through the funnel, where they will be trapped in the top container.

Take a Closer Look

Below are some of the flies and insects you might catch in your insect trap.

Housefly *(Musca domestica)*

• Attracted to: manure, garbage, rotting fruits and vegetables

• House flies lay eggs on wet organic matter such as moist garbage. The eggs hatch into maggots that feed on the garbage until they change into pupae and, finally, adult flies. It takes about two weeks for eggs to become flies, depending on the temperature.

Blowfly *(Calliphoridae)*

• Attracted to: dead animals, garbage

• Blowflies come in shiny, metallic colors of copper, green, blue, or black. These flies lay their eggs on the carcases of dead animals or decaying meat. They have a very predictable life cycle from maggot to adult fly and are quite useful to forensic entomologists for determining time of death in murder cases.

Fruit fly *(Drosophila)*

• Attracted to: garbage, rotting fruits and vegetables, drains and sewers

• Fruit flies are also known as pomace flies or vinegar flies. They are very small with red eyes. Since they're mostly attracted to rotting fruits and vegetables, they're not much help in analyzing dead bodies. They will help you find the apple you left in your locker before it turns to mush, though.

Phorid fly *(Phoridae)*

• Attracted to: garbage, rotting fruits and vegetables, drains and sewers

• Phorid flies or humpbacked flies are very small, dark brown to almost black, and move in a jerky manner. Phorid flies are often mistaken for fruit flies. They're almost identical, except their eyes are black instead of red.

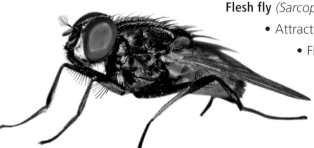

Flesh fly *(Sarcophagidae)*

• Attracted to: dead animals, garbage

• Flesh flies are gray with black stripes. They are usually the first insects to arrive at a dead animal. As with the blowfly, the development of flesh fly larvae can be used to pinpoint the time of death.

Try This!

The Life Cycle of Maggots

Observe the life cycle of maggots by watching them grow. Put a piece of meat in an open jar and leave it outside for an hour or two on a warm day so that flies can find the meat and lay eggs. Cover the jar and punch three small holes in the lid to let in air, and secure it tightly. In about a day you'll notice small maggots crawling on the meat and, in around a week, they'll change into pupae and then into flies. Keep track of when the changes occur. Try changing the conditions, such as temperature, humidity, and light, and observe the effects on the maggot life cycle.

Warning: If possible, store the jar outside, as it will get quite stinky..

Explore Further

Try other baits in the insect trap to see what types of insects are attracted. Adjust other variables such as temperature, humidity, time of day, or light. You can even test the saying, "You catch more flies with honey than vinegar."

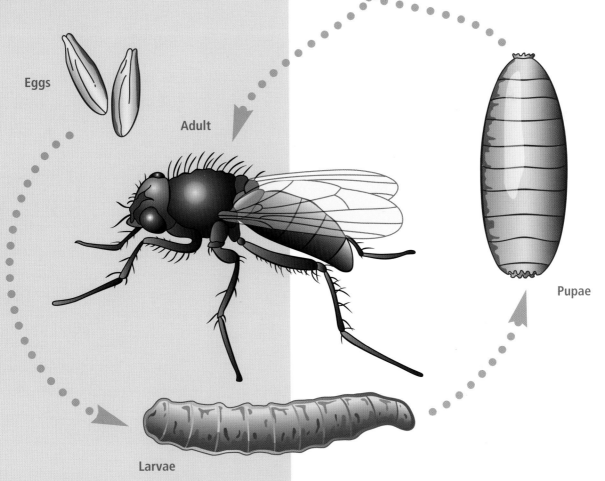

Eggs

Adult

Pupae

Larvae

Flame Test

Most chemicals are complicated molecules made up of several basic elements. A flame test is one tool that forensic chemists use to identify some of the elements in a chemical and ultimately the chemical. Identifying a poison or drug can be crucial in solving a crime, especially if it proves a suspect is innocent.

Safety Warning:

Perform this experiment in a well-ventilated area with an adult present. Wear goggles. Do not attempt to burn salts or chemicals that are not listed in this experiment. Do not eat or taste any of the chemicals.

Problem

How does the type of metal in a chemical affect the color produced when it's heated in a flame?

Experiment Summary

You'll heat different metals in a flame and observe the colors produced.

What You Need

- ○ Safety goggles
- ○ Water
- ○ Measuring spoons
- ○ 90 percent Isopropyl (rubbing) alcohol
- ○ Cups
- ○ Extra-long cotton swabs
- ○ Candle
- ○ Matches
- ○ Table salt (sodium chloride)
- ○ Salt substitute (potassium chloride)*
- ○ De-icer (calcium chloride)*
- ○ Pool algecide (copper chloride or copper sulfate)*
- ○ Powdered roach killer (boric acid)
- ○ Cream of tartar (potassium bitartrate)
- ○ Plaster of Paris (calcium sulfate)
- ○ Mortar and pestle (optional)

Check the labels of these products to make sure they contain the chemical listed here.

Experimental Procedure

1. It's best to perform this experiment outside. If it's too windy to keep the candle lit, find a well-ventilated room and open a few windows before beginning this experiment. Keep a glass cup or ceramic mug full of water nearby. (You'll use this to extinguish flames.)

2. Pour 1 tablespoon (15 ml) of rubbing alcohol into a cup. Dip one end of the cotton swab in the alcohol so that the cotton is completely soaked. Rubbing alcohol is very flammable, so put the lid on it and move the bottle at least 6 feet (1.8 m) away from the place where you're burning the candle.

3. Light the candle. Quickly pass the alcohol-soaked end of the cotton swab through the flame of the candle. The alcohol will catch on fire and burn like a tiny torch. Carefully observe the colors of the flame. Is the color at the top of the flame the same as the part right near the cotton swab? Notice that the cotton is not burning or turning black. The alcohol will burn before the cotton or the rest of the swab starts to burn. Be sure to blow out the flame when this starts to happen! Drop the cotton swab in the glass of water if you need to. Do not drop the burning cotton swab in the alcohol! Record your observations.

4. In another cup, mix 1 tablespoon (15 ml) of alcohol with 1 tablespoon (.5 oz) of table salt.

5. Stir the cotton swab in the mixture until the end is completely coated with the salt and alcohol mixture. Repeat step 3. Observe the colors of the flame and how they are different from what you saw in step 3. After a few seconds, you will see sparks and flashes near the bottom and along the outside edges of the flame. Then the entire flame will change to a bright orange-yellow before it slowly burns out. Record your observations, particularly the color of the flame. Don't forget to blow out the flame when the cotton swab starts burning.

6. Repeat steps 4 and 5 for the other chemicals. If the chemicals don't dissolve well in the alcohol, use a mortar and pestle or a spoon to crush the salt into smaller pieces.

Conclusion

The metal atoms in the chemicals cause the colors produced in the flame. In this experiment, the metals you used are sodium, potassium, calcium, copper, and boron. What colors did these metals produce? Compare the two chemicals that contain potassium (cream of tartar and salt substitute) and calcium (de-icer and plaster of Paris). How were the flames similar and how were they different? Could you identify the chemicals based on the flame's color?

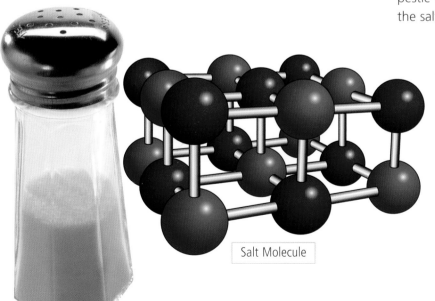

Salt Molecule

Take a Closer Look

To understand how these chemicals produce different color flames, you first need to look at how an atom works.

Every atom has a nucleus, made of protons and neutrons, surrounded by electrons. We are mainly concerned with the electrons in this case. Different atoms, like sodium or potassium, have different numbers of electrons. These electrons spin and move about the nucleus very, very fast (faster than you could even imagine, much less see) and the electrons have different, but very specific, energy levels like steps on a staircase. When an atom gains energy from heat or light, the electrons will jump up to a higher step. However, the electrons eventually have to come back down to their original energy level. When they do, they give up the energy in the form of light. The color of the light depends on how big a step the electron took. Red, orange, and yellow light have less energy than green, blue, and violet light and indicate smaller steps. The size of the steps, and therefore the color given off, depends on the atom. This is why sodium gives off a bright orange-yellow color and potassium gives a violet flame.

In this experiment, you don't actually "burn" the chemicals. The rubbing alcohol burns and the chemicals are heated to a very high temperature. The metal ions of the chemicals (sodium, potassium, calcium, copper, and boron) absorb this heat energy, and the electrons in these metal ions get excited, or raised to a higher energy level.

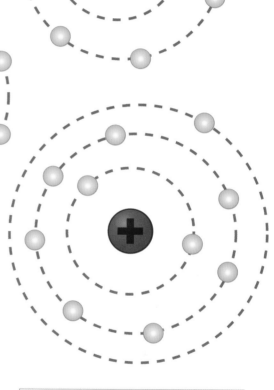

3. The excited electron falls back down, releasing its energy as a packet of red light.

1. Neon atom in a neon light bulb.

2. Lights on! As the atom is heated, one of the electrons jumps to a higher evergy level.

Try This!

Build a Spectrometer

The colors seen in the flames are a combination of all the colors emitted by the electrons when they are raised to a higher energy level by the heat of the flame and then fall back down. With a spectroscope, you can see these individual colors. For example, the color produced when you heated the boric acid was green. If you looked at the same flame with a spectroscope, you'd see that the green is actually caused by a combination of yellow and blue (with a little bit of red).

The bright lines on the CD below show the spectrum of colors given off when the electrons fall down off the "step" they jumped up to when the heat energy was added.

What You Need

- Scissors
- Black construction paper
- Ruler
- Shoebox
- A CD that you don't need anymore
- Black electrical tape

What You Do

1. Use the scissors to cut two pieces from the black construction paper 2 inches by 3 inches (5 x 7.6 cm) in size.

2. On the top of the shoebox, cut a slit that is 2 inches (5 cm) long, about ½ inch (1 cm) from the end of the box.

3. Tape the two pieces of black construction paper over the slit so that the papers are almost, but not quite, touching. There should be a very narrow (about ¹⁄₁₆ inch [.16 cm]) slit between the papers for the light to come through.

4. Cut a viewing hole about 1-inch square on the opposite end of the box. This is where you'll look to see the spectra.

5. Tape the CD, shiny side up, inside the box under the slit so that it makes a 60-degree angle with the bottom of the box. The light that enters through the slit will bounce off of the CD and out the viewing hole to your eyes. The grooves in the CD spread the light out into all of its colors so you can see in the spectrometer which colors make up the colors seen in the flames.

6. To use the spectrometer, turn off all of the lights so the room is dark, and have a helper light a cotton swab with one of the chemicals as in step 5 of the experiment. Hold the spectrometer so the flame is in front of the slit. Look through the viewing hole to see the spectrum or colors of the flame. You may need to make adjustments to the angle of the CD to get the best view of the spectrum.

How are the spectra for the different flames similar and how are they different? Do you see just one band of color or several? Try using the spectrometer to view other light sources, like sunlight, fluorescent lights, and neon lights.

Fibers & Fabric

Everywhere you go, you leave fibers—from your clothing, for example. And you pick up fibers from carpets, furniture, and the places you visit. In 1910, a criminologist named Edmond Locard came up with a theory to describe this phenomenon that states, "Every contact leaves a trace." This means that every time something comes in contact with another thing, it either takes or leaves something. Forensic scientists look carefully at fibers found at crime scenes to help figure out who a criminal or victim is and where they've been. One method for identifying fibers is to observe how they burn.

Problem

How do different fabrics burn?

Experiment Summary

You'll observe different types of fabric as they burn.

What You Need

- ◯ Tweezers or forceps
- ◯ Fibers or threads from wool, rayon, silk, polyester, and cotton (dark-colored fabrics work best)
- ◯ White paper
- ◯ Black paper
- ◯ Magnifying glass
- ◯ Candle
- ◯ Matches
- ◯ Microscope (optional)
- ◯ Glass slide and slip cover (optional)

Explore Further

Try burning a larger piece of fabric instead of a single thread. What other types of fabric can you test? Try nylon, acetate, and spandex. Can you identify an unknown fiber from the way it burns? Put a clean bag in a vacuum cleaner and vacuum a small area of your house. Remove the bag and use the tweezers to explore what's inside. What types of fibers do you find? Can you identify where these fibers came from?

Experimental Procedure

1. Use the tweezers to place a single fiber or thread of fabric on a piece of paper. If the thread is light-colored, place it on the black paper. If it's dark-colored, place it on the white paper.

2. Examine the fiber carefully with the magnifying glass. Make a sketch of what you see and record your observations, including its shape, size, and color.

3. Repeat steps 1 and 2 for each type of fabric.

4. If you have access to a microscope, place the fiber on a glass slide. Add a drop of water and cover it with a slipcover. View the fiber under a microscope and record or sketch your observations.

5. Light the candle and hold one of the fibers with the tweezers. As you bring the fiber near the flame, observe what happens. Does it melt, curl, or catch fire? Record your observations.

6. Bring the fiber into the flame. Does it light slowly or quickly? Does it melt, flicker, or pop? Record your observations.

7. Remove the fiber from the flame. Does it go out by itself, continue to burn, smoke, or glow? Do you smell any odor from the burning fiber? What does the fiber look like after you remove it? What do the ashes look like? Use the magnifying glass to examine the burnt fiber more closely. Record your observations.

8. Repeat steps 5 through 7 three times for each fabric.

Conclusion

Rayon and polyester are man-made fibers. Cotton, silk, and wool are natural fibers. How did the behavior of the man-made fibers compare to the natural fibers when burned? How did the fibers compare when examined under the microscope? What are some advantages and disadvantages of using this method to identify fibers?

Take a Closer Look

Fabrics or fibers can be classified as either natural or man-made. You can identify which type of fabric it is by carefully observing the way it burns.

The most common natural fabrics include cotton, wool, and silk. Cotton is made from the cotton plant and is mostly cellulose. (Cellulose also makes up trees and paper.) Therefore, cotton will burn and smolder, much like paper, with a large flame that consumes all of the fabric or fiber. Wool is just sheep hair spun into yarn, so it smells like hair as it burns. The ash left by wool forms small balls along the edge of the fabric. Silk is collected from silkworms. (They spin it to make their cocoons.) It burns with a very small flame but also smells like burnt hair and leaves a black, shiny ash.

Man-made or synthetic fabrics include rayon, nylon, and polyester. Scientists design these fabrics in a laboratory for specific properties, such as texture or durability. Rayon is one of the few synthetic fibers made from cellulose, the same natural material as in cotton. Therefore rayon burns the same way that cotton does. The type of rayon determines how much ash is produced.

Other synthetic materials, such as nylon and polyester, melt instead of burning. Melted black or brown blobs are left along the edge of the fabric afterward. These fabrics are made of polymers, or long chains of molecules that are more like plastics than natural fibers. Since they don't burn, the burn test can only be used to determine that a fabric is a polymer synthetic, but not the specific type.

Recycle This!

Next time you pull on your fuzzy, warm fleece jacket think about this: In the not-too-distant past, someone drank soda out of your shirt. If you don't want your plastic bottle to spend 450 years in the landfill, recycle it! Recycled plastic bottles can be turned into polyester fleece. Clear-colored bottles are made into light-colored fleece and green bottles are turned into darker-colored fleece. One recycled fleece jacket can use as many as 25 plastic bottles to make.

Fleece and plastic bottles have the same molecular structure; they're both polymers! Polymers are a chain of individual molecules bound together in long lines. There are many, many types of polymers. Fleece, plastic, gum, duct tap, and many other things are synthetic polymers. Naturally occurring polymers include wood, leather, cotton, and rubber.

If you link a bunch of paper clips together, you've got a reasonable approximation of what a polymer chain looks like. Each of the paper clips is like a single molecule (called a monomer). The monomers link together end to end to form a polymer chain.

The polymer chains cross-link (attach to the other polymer chains next to them) a little bit, but the cross-link bond is nowhere near as strong as the links between the monomers in the polymer chain. If you try to rip a plastic grocery bag, you'll notice that pulling it one way stretches the bag. You're pulling the polymer chains in the direction that they lie, so they stretch out. If you pull the other way, the bag will rip because you're pulling the polymer chains apart from the other polymer chains where they aren't bonded together as tightly. If you rip a piece of newspaper, a similar thing happens because newspaper is made of wood, a naturally occurring polymer.

Glossary

Abstract. The part of your project report which gives an overview of your experiment.

Accidental characteristics. Cuts, wear patterns, and other marks that make a shoe or tool mark unique.

Accurate. Measurements that are close to the true or real value.

Anthropometrics. Using body measurements to identify people.

Apparatus. A piece of equipment, tool, or instrument that you use to perform your experiment.

Average. A number that is typical or representative of a set of numbers.

Blood spatter pattern. The pattern made by droplets of blood.

Blood type. Any of the four main kinds of human blood (O, A, B, AB).

Body language. Communication through facial expressions, gestures, and postures.

Cell. The basic unit of living matter.

Chromatograph. The separation of a substance into its components.

Chromosome. A small body present in all living cells that carries genes which determine hereditary traits.

Clot. When the solid parts of blood clump together, stopping blood from continuing to flow.

Compression. Pushing force.

Control. Something that stays the same throughout your experiment.

Cyanoacrylate fuming method. A reliable, easy, and inexpensive way to record fingerprints using glue.

Data. The measurements you take or information you gather.

Decay. The way memories weaken as time passes.

Dependent variable. The thing that changes as a result of changes made to the independent variable.

DNA pen. A pen that mixes saliva into the ink to authenticate the signature and protect people from forgery.

Deoxyribonucleic Acid (DNA). An acid found in living cells that forms the main part of chromosomes.

Dust for fingerprints. A method in which you use dust to record fingerprints.

Encoding. The first stage of memory storage.

Enzymes. Proteins produced by living cells that act as catalysts in biochemical reactions.

Exemplars. Handwriting samples of known origin.

Fingerprint. An impression formed by the skin on the tip of the finger.

Forensics. The use of science to investigate and establish facts for use in a court of law.

Friction ridge skin. The ridges and furrows in the skin on your hands and feet.

Gait pattern. The unique way a person walks.

Genes. DNA segments that determine hereditary characteristics.

Graphology. A pseudoscience that supposedly reveals personality through handwriting.

Hydrophilic. A molecule that is attracted to water.

Hydrophobic. A molecule that is repelled by water.

Hypothesis. An educated guess at the answer to your question.

Independent variable. The thing that you change in an experiment.

Index of refraction. A measurement of how much glass bends light, used to identify types of glass.

Interference. When an eyewitness' memory is altered by someone asking leading questions.

Jaccard's index. A method that studies insects to determine the similarity of two different locations.

Latent prints. A print made by sweat and oil that is invisible to the naked eye.

Molded prints. 3-dimensional prints that are left in a soft substance.

Nominal. When your data are names or things rather than numbers.

Nucleus. The structure inside of a cell that contains the DNA.

Ordinal. When your data are numbers.

Outliers. Weird data points that don't fit in with the rest of your measurements.

Physical anthropology. The study of the human body, particularly bones.

Plastic prints. See molded prints.

Polygraph. A machine that records data from different physical systems while a person is answering questions.

Polymerase chain reaction (PCR). A test performed on blood to find out to whom it belongs.

Polymers. A compound made of many simple molecules linked together.

Precipitating. The condensation of a solid from a liquid.

Precise. Measurements that are close to each other.

Random error. When factors out of your control cause different measurements.

Ratio. A numerical description of the relationship between two things.

Restriction fragment length polymorphisms (RFLP). A test performed on the DNA found in blood to figure out whom it belongs to.

Retrieval. The ability to access a stored memory.

Scientific method. A set of guidelines scientists use to help them answer questions.

Serum. The yellowish liquid that remains after the proteins in blood have clotted.

Shearing. When two surfaces are pulled in opposite directions.

Slope. The description of how much a line slants, mathematically expressed as rise divided by run.

Storage. How a witness keeps the details of a memory in his mind.

Systematic error. An error cause by doing the same thing wrong every time.

Tension. A pulling force.

Trials. The number of times you perform part of your experiment with the same conditions.

Tuberosity. The knob at the end of a bone.

Viscosity. The amount of flow a liquid has.

Visible print. A finger or footprint made with ink, blood, mud, or another substance that is easy to see.

Acknowledgments

Thanks to everyone who made this book possible, especially:
Sam and Geoff Harris, Rose McLarney, Steve Mann, Orrin Lundgren, Lawrence Hines, Bradley Norris, Susan Kieffer, Marcus Moses, Jack LeGwin, and all the participants in North Carolina's local, regional, and state fairs. This book couldn't have been done without you!

Index